THE EGLINTON TOURNAMENT OF 1839

Text by the Reverend John Richardson
Illustrations by James Henry Nixon
First published by Colnaghi and Puckle, London 1843

Royal Armouries facsimile reprint 2009

Royal Armouries Museum
Armouries Drive
Leeds LS10 1LT

ISBN 978-0-948092-61-9
Printed in Great Britain by BAS Fine Art Printers, Amesbury, Wiltshire

The Eglintoun Tournament **in 1839**
Puckle (late Colnaghi and Puckle)

This is one of the most beautiful works
that has been published from some time, and
forms a splendid book for the drawing-
room table. It consists of twenty-two
plates, from drawings taken on the spot
by Mr. Nixon, lithographed by Aubrey
and Loiellot, and accompanied by
historical and descriptive notices from the
pen of the Rev. J. Richardson, LL.D., &c.
The points are elaborately coloured; great
care being taken faithfully to delineate the
dazzling pageantry of the tournament.
Around each print, forming a border, is a
very appropriate design, which greatly en-
riches the work. The letter-press is highly
illuminated. The first fourteen plates
consist of the procession to the lists, which
are as follows:- Earl of Eglintoun, with
body guard, Knight Marshal, King of the
Tournament, Queen of Beauty, Lord of
the Tournament, Knight of the Griffin
and Dragon, Knight of the Lion, &c.;
general view of the lists, the challenge, the
joust, the *melee*, the presentation, the
banquet, the ball, &c., &c. This work
must be seen to be properly appreciated.
and we only wonder, how such a book
can be offered for ten guineas.

The Mirror, Saturday 3 February, 1844

CONTENTS

THE EGLINTON TOURNAMENT AND THE REVIVAL OF CHIVALRY

In 1839 '*I gave a tournament at Eglinton*'. With this stunning understatement, Lord Eglinton, in his memoirs, passed over the event that has made his name famous. It was an event that was intended to be the most magnificent and glorious expression of the revival of chivalry.

Archibald William Montgomerie was born in Palermo in 1812 where his father, Archibald, Lord Montgomerie, was a diplomat at the court of the King of Sicily. His father died when he was only two years old, and his grandfather, Hugh Montgomerie, 12th Earl of Eglinton, was appointed his guardian. The young Archibald spent the next few years living with his grandfather at Eglinton Castle and during that time was strongly influenced by the old man's love of history. When his grandfather died in 1819, Archibald became the 13th Earl of Eglinton, but until he came of age the responsibility for the management of the estate fell to a nominated board of trustees.

As a young man Eglinton was a keen sportsman. He loved archery, and was made Captain of the Ancient Society of Kilwinning Archers in 1825 (the local archers were present at the Eglinton Tournament as the Irvine Toxophilites and the Ballochmyle Archeresses). In the winter he played curling, and had two curling ponds in Eglinton Park; in the summer he played bowls and golf. He ensured that there was a bowling green in every village on his estates, and was a founder of the North Berwick Golf Club in 1832 (along with his friend and neighbour, Captain Fairlie, who appeared as the Knight of the Golden Lion at the tournament).

Eglinton was particularly keen on horse racing. He was famous as a racehorse owner and breeder, and a member of the Jockey Club. His horses won the St Leger three times and the Derby once. He staged three-day race meetings at his own racecourse at Eglinton Park and in 1839, just six months before the tournament, he staged the first four-mile steeplechases ever held in Scotland.

Figure 1 *Studies for the portrait of Lord Douglas, Lord Stradbroke and Lord Eglinton in 'The Waterloo Cup Coursing Meeting', 1840 (oil on board), by Richard Ansdell.*
© *Yale Centre for British Art, Paul Mellon Centre, USA/Bridgeman Art Library*

It may have been his love of history and equestrian sports that first gave him the idea of holding a medieval tournament. At a dinner held in his honour by the inhabitants of Irvine on 29 September 1839, Eglinton claimed that:

'*I have long looked back at the age of chivalry with admiration, and regretted that the sports which distinguished it, as well as the courtesy and high feeling which were the principal features of the knightly character, now existed only in the pages of history, or the legends of romance. I have poured, when a boy, over the exploits of King Arthur, and the Knights of the Round Table ... In my later years, I have pondered over the pages of Froissart... and I have awoke from my dream of chivalry, to find myself in a more refined, but a most unromantic age… Can it be wondered at that I endeavoured to realize what was the dream of my boyhood, and the admiration of my riper years.'* [1]

In fact Eglinton may have originally intended nothing more than a few medieval games to enliven his annual race meeting, but the idea was taken up by the *Court Journal* and spread like wildfire even firing the Earl himself with enthusiasm. Eglinton's intentions may have been partly political. As a staunch Tory he would have disapproved of the Whig's Reform Bill and also their cancellation of some of the traditional festivities at the coronation of Queen Victoria, including that of throwing down of the gauntlet of the Queen's Champion. His own stepfather, Sir Charles Lamb, was the hereditary Knight Marshal of the Royal Household, and was denied the opportunity to officiate at the coronation when the government decided to simplify and limit the pageantry of the ceremony. As a private individual Eglinton was giving a public entertainment, which the government was unwilling to do, and at the same time reaffirming his belief in the English class structure. But much of this political intent was read into the event afterwards. At no time did Eglinton make a political statement.

The revival of chivalry

In the late 18th century there was a revival in interest in the Middle Ages. This rediscovery manifested itself in literature, in the architecture of country houses and castles, and in the insatiable interest in collecting arms and armour to decorate homes with antiquities from the 'Age of Chivalry'. The first two books devoted exclusively to the study of the historical development of arms and armour were published at this time; J B L Carre's *Panoplie* published in 1785 (in French) and F Grose's *Treatise on Ancient Armour and Weapons* in 1786.

A major influence in the development of the Gothic Revival was Horace Walpole, the youngest son of the British Prime Minister Robert Walpole. In 1748 he bought a villa at Strawberry Hill near Twickenham, and within a few years he had turned it into a Gothic castle. Although this wasn't the first gothicised castle of the Revival, it was, in the public's eye, the most memorable. This was due in large part to Walpole's position in society and his large circle of acquaintances that visited and commented on Strawberry Hill. He filled the house with a great many medieval antiquities including much arms and armour. He purchased the so-called 'Francois I' suit at the Crozat sale in 1772 (now in the Metropolitan Museum of Art, New York) and bought much of the arms and armour at the Comte de Caylus sale in 1773.

Walpole also wrote the first of the so-called 'Gothick' novels; *The Castle of Otranto* which was first published in 1765. Walpole wrote it, as he recorded in the preface, after he dreamed of a gigantic hand in armour crashing onto the stairs at Strawberry Hill. Set in the 12th century, it is filled with knights, castles, ghosts and combats. However, although these Gothic novels used the settings of the Middle Ages, it was primarily as a device to provide appropriately menacing and thrilling settings for tales of terror.

Figure 2
Engraving of the North Front of Strawberry Hill, Twickenham, 1784.
© *Guildhall Library, City of London/Bridgeman Art Library*

It was on the foundations of the Gothic Revival that Walter Scott built the second stage of the Romantic Movement when he combined romance and history, fusing the ideal and the real. He introduced a new element taken from 13th-century troubadour ballads. This was the code of chivalric values. The first of these romances was *Ivanhoe* written in 1820, which told the story of a Saxon knight returning to England after the Third Crusade, and included a description of a medieval tournament held at Ashby de la Zouch. The book and the tournament were sources of inspiration to artists and scenes from *Ivanhoe* appeared regularly at exhibitions. In 1838, when Eglinton announced his tournament, Thomas Allom's *The tournament at Ashby de la Zouch* was being exhibited at the Royal Academy.

Figure 3
Engraving of the Tournament at Ashby de la Zouche, after Thomas Allom
© *Edinburgh University Library*

Exhibitions and Samuel Luke Pratt
Thus there was in art, literature and architecture a mood inspired by the Middle Ages and the code of chivalry, and this was reflected by a great desire to see the antiquities of the past. Arms and armour could of course be seen at the Tower of London where the old royal armoury had been set up in the 17th century, but these were badly organised and not displayed in any historical manner. In 1825 the Board of Ordnance invited Sir Samuel Rush Meyrick to rearrange the collection at the Tower of London in the new Horse Armoury. The previous year Meyrick had published his *Critical Inquiry in Ancient Armour*, which was the first book to provide a chronological survey based on a study of early documents, illustrations and some actual pieces of armour. He stressed the importance of English monarch by viewing historical periods in terms of their reigns. Meyrick re-arranged the armours in the Tower in an historical sequence which became known as the 'Line of Kings'.

While arms and armour could be seen at the Tower they could be bought at exhibitions held in London by Thomas Gwennap and his successor Samuel Luke Pratt. Pratt became the largest dealer in London having premises at four different addresses in the city. He was primarily a dealer in arms and armour, however he was also listed in the trade directories as '*Upholsterer*', '*Trunk and Packing Case Manufacturer*' and later as '*Cabinet Maker*' and '*Importer of Ancient Furniture*'. He took great care with the displays of his exhibitions. For the refurbishment of his showroom at 3 Lower Grosvenor Street, he employed L N

4

Cottingham, famous for his gothic Snelston Hall in Derbyshire (1827). He designed for Pratt a *truly Gothic Apartment*.[2] It was at this showroom that Pratt held an *'Exhibition of Ancient Arms and Armour'* in 1838. The preface in the catalogue of his exhibition summarises public feeling at the time:

'The rapid growth of a taste for Literature and Fine Arts, which the last half century has developed, as well in this country as in the continental nations of Europe, has naturally been productive of an increased spirit of research into the manners and institutions, civil and military, of our ancestors. There is nothing to enquirers of this class (and perhaps to the public generally) more illustrative and interesting than Collections of the Armour and Weapons of that period of bygone time, known as the Middle Ages. To gaze on the plumed casque of the Mailed Knight equipped for the Tournament, and to grasp the ponderous mace, yet encrusted with the accumulated rust of centuries, cannot fail to inspire admiration of the chivalrous deeds of our ancestors.'

Pratt was entrusted by Eglinton with all of the detailed arrangements for the tournament, and the first meeting of 150 prospective participants was held at his Bond Street showroom.

The relevance of history and chivalry
The ideals of chivalry were not dreams of a bygone age of romance, good manners and idealised love. Actually, the Victorians considered the Middle Ages to be an exemplum to follow for their modern lives. This included living in a society where everyone looked after each other as in a brotherhood (fraternity) and also cared for the poor and oppressed. These were very modern concerns and they saw in King Arthur and the Knights of the Round Table, for example, an inspiration for how they should live their lives. One of the Eglinton authors [Anon] summarises this point superbly:

'Having allowed my mind to revert to the often obscurely written annals of past ages, methinks that I can see, through the dark glass of history, those assembled knights linked together by the bonds of the strictest fraternity, and supported by their king, round one vast mysterious table, reciting their past deed of valour, or forming fresh schemes of future achievement; again, I fancy that I can see them after having dispersed themselves throughout the nation, ever seeking to efface foul outrage, to right and succour the oppressed, for these were the fundamental principles of their laws.'[3]

The Victorians were much concerned with the ills of modern society and looked to the past with the understanding that a study of history could teach much about human behaviour and endeavour. Anon stresses this point directly:

'I must now beg to remind my readers that many of the greatest comforts and blessings that are enjoyed by us of the present generation, were obtained and confirmed by the chivalry and generous valour of our forefathers, - that chivalry is not placed in opposition to the institutions of nations, but that it arises from a feeling of honour interspersed throughout society without disturbing it, and is ever striving to improve the various orders of the state; that with its rise arose civilisation, and that with its rise the fairer portion of the creation ceased to be slaves, and became equals, and then idols, often stimulation to deeds of the most heroic patriotism.'[4]

The Eglinton Tournament thus epitomised the mood of the time. It is difficult now to look back and imagine the excitement that was aroused at the very thought of a tournament. To many it was the culmination of the Gothic Revival of Horace Walpole and the Romantic Movement of Walter Scott, which had begun more than fifty years earlier.

A BRIEF DESCRIPTION OF THE EGLINTON TOURNAMENT

The tournament was set to take place at Eglinton Castle in Ayrshire on the 28 and 29 August 1839. The castle, situated on the banks of the river Lugton, about a mile southeast of Kilwinning and half a mile north of the small town of Irvine, had been rebuilt in 1796 by Hugh Montgomerie, the 12th Earl of Eglinton (the paternal grandfather of Lord Eglinton). The house was a magnificent castellated edifice in the gothic style, and was described in *The Topographical, Statistical and Historical Gazeteer of Scotland* (1848):

'There is a large round keep and at the corners are circular turrets joined together by a curtain - to use the language of fortification. The whole is pierced with modern windows, which in some degree destroy the castellated effect, but add to the internal comfort. The interior of the fabric corresponds with the magnitude and beauty of its exterior. From a spacious entrance hall, a saloon opens, 36 feet in diameter, the whole height of the edifice, and lighted from above; and from this the principal rooms enter. All the apartments are spacious, well-lighted and furnished and adorned in the most superb manner. One of them in the front is 52 feet long, 32 wide, and 24 from floor to ceiling. Every thing about the castle contributes to an imposing display of splendid elegance and refined taste. Nor are the lawns around it less admired for their fine woods, and varied surfaces, and beautiful scenery. The park round the castle is 1200 acres in extent, and has one-third of its area in plantation.'

Shortly after the first rumours of the tournament appeared in the *Court Journal* (4 August 1838), Eglinton held a meeting of 150 prospective knights at Samuel Pratt's showroom in Bond Street. Pratt was a key figure from the very beginning, and Eglinton entrusted him with all of the arrangements:

'The details of the preparations were confided to Messrs. Pratt of Bond Street, who, from their acquaintance with ancient armour, their knowledge of the nature and use of ancient weapons, and their established reputation in the ordering of all ancient decorations, were better qualified than any other individuals in the kingdom to do justice to the conceptions of the noble earl, by whom their knowledge and talents were put into requisition.'[5]

Most of the participants, at least those not intimidated by the cost, naturally looked to Pratt to supply the necessary armours and costumes for themselves and their retinues. Some of the armours may have included genuine 16th-century pieces, but most were 19th-century reproductions probably made by the armourer, Thomas Grimshaw. Many of the costumes came from Haigh, a well known London theatrical costumier.

Figure 4
Engraving of the Tilt Yard near Regent's Park, after Waterhouse Hawkins © Board of Trustees of the Armouries

Figure 5
Captain Maynard's invitation to the rehearsals
© Board of Trustees of the Armouries

In the last few months before the tournament Pratt organised practices in a garden behind the Eyre Arms Tavern, close to Regent's Park. When the final dress rehearsal took place on 13 July the initial 35 knights had been reduced to nineteen. Interest in the tournament had now reached fever pitch. The public's *'curiosity was excited to its highest degree, and great interest was made to obtain tickets of admission to behold the feats to be performed'.*[6] As many as 6,000 people attended, and the event was well supported by London society. Amongst the audience were the Duchess of Beaufort, the Marquis of Worcester, Lord Augustus Somerset, Lord Fitzroy Somerset, and the Dowager Duchess of Richmond.

The practices had gone well, except for one. In the first rehearsal John Campbell of Saddell was jousting when his opponent's lance glanced off his breastplate and struck his right shoulder. Campbell was not wearing any arm defences, and so received a nasty wound. Following the incident there was a brisk correspondence between Eglinton and the Sheriff of Ayr about the safety of the tournament. The Sheriff held the view that should an accidental death occur, then the person responsible for inflicting the wound could be charged with homicide. Eglinton assured the Sheriff that all precautions were being taken:

'The armour has been most carefully examined; no one will be allowed to tilt in armour that has not been inspected by the person whom I have intrusted the management of the tournament; and all the defensive armour will be worn which could be worn even were we going to engage in a combat a l'outrance.

The lances are only poles, quite round at the end, and without points. They are not too strong; and they are made of the cross-grain of the wood, so that they cannot splinter. It is therefore impossible that any one can be hurt, either by the blow of the lance, or by its entering any of the crevices of the armour; and the only danger to be apprehended is the chance of a fall'.[7]

In a conflict of interests that would not be permitted today, Pratt was entrusted with inspecting the armour which in most cases he had actually supplied. Nevertheless the prospect of danger only seems to have further increased public interest in the event. Eglinton, encouraged by Pratt, had offered free tickets to the tournament to the readers of *The Times*, the *Morning Post* and the *Court Gazette*, and local newspapers all over the country had repeated his offer. He was overwhelmed with applications. Henry Curling, an officer of the 52nd Regiment on half pay *'found the Eglintoun tournament haunted my imagination'* and was determined to make the journey to Scotland *'despite an ill-state of health'*.[8] He set out from his home in Surrey on Tuesday 20 August, and the following day took a steam train from London to Birmingham and then on to Liverpool. From there he crossed by sea to Ardrossan in Ayrshire on a boat especially engaged to provide transport for the tournament. Travelling with him were all manner of passengers and equipment destined for Eglinton Castle, including *'divers artisans from London… half a squadron of chargers for the knights, esquires and attendants… cooks eager to ply their art for the banqueting scene… artists to perpetuate the prowess of the champions… swordsmen, and gentlemen of the press'*, and last but not least *'several of the knights, and their esquires and pages'*.[9] After landing at Ardrossan, Curling took a horse-drawn carriage, and finally arrived in Irvine on the morning of 26 August. In his excitement he determined to visit the castle immediately, and *'guided by the clink of hammers, I soon reached the object of my search, the Listed Fields'*. He was delighted to find that *'The ground, like that described by Sir Walter in his account of the Passage of Arms at Ashby, was as if fashioned on purpose for the martial encounter'*. [10]

Curling then walked back to Irvine, where he found the small town overwhelmed by thousands of visitors, many of whom were struggling to find accommodation. In the days leading up to the event the Glasgow newspapers advised their readers that:

''In Kilwinning, which is little more than a mile from the grounds, there is no accommodation, and we believe that Irvine, which is two miles distant, is nearly, if not wholly engaged. Kilmarnock is eight miles, and many may find accommodation there; while, in a difficulty, a vast number will likely go off by the steam-train, just established, to Ayr, which is only 12 miles off.' [11]

Tuesday 27 August

On the day before the tournament, many people took the opportunity to visit the castle. They took great delight in simply walking the grounds and the deer park, to which they did not normally have access. *'All were permitted to come and go, prowl about, look upon every thing going on and amuse themselves as they liked'*. [12] The visitors found the castle a hive of activity, and the library:

'presented a scene over which Mars, attended by the Cyclops, might have presided. And there was Mr. Pratt, and with him thirty assistants, unpacking ponderous cases – drawing forth the casque, the cuirass, the battle-axe and brand, the gonfalon and gauntlet, the spur and spear. Around crowded impatient knights and right trusty squires…'. [13]

The castle was too small for all of the guests that Eglinton had invited, and so a temporary pavilion, about 375 feet long and 45 feet wide, had been constructed at the rear of the castle, and linked to it by a grand staircase. This building was divided into three rooms: the middle room formed a large reception area, the room on the left was a ballroom and the room on the right was a banqueting hall:

'Over the archways of the ball and banquet rooms were the arms of Eglinton. The proscenium was adorned also with evergreens and variegated lamps, surrounded by the union flag of England. The whole, covered with canvas and lined with crimson and white calico, presented an appearance at once spacious and elegant'. [14]

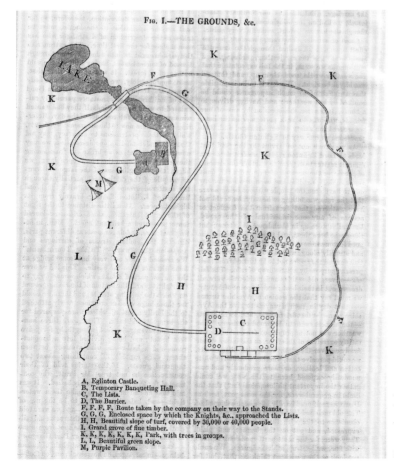

FIG. I.—THE GROUNDS, &c.

A, Eglinton Castle.
B, Temporary Banqueting Hall.
C, The Lists.
D, The Barrier.
F, F, F, F, Route taken by the company on their way to the Stands.
G, G, G, Enclosed space by which the Knights, &c., approached the Lists.
H, H, Beautiful slope of turf, covered by 30,000 or 40,000 people.
I, Grand grove of fine timber.
K, K, K, K, K, K, K, Park, with trees in groups.
L, L, Beautiful green slope.
M, Purple Pavilion.

Figure 6

Plan of the grounds of Eglinton Castle, from Tait's Edinburgh Magazine (November 1839)

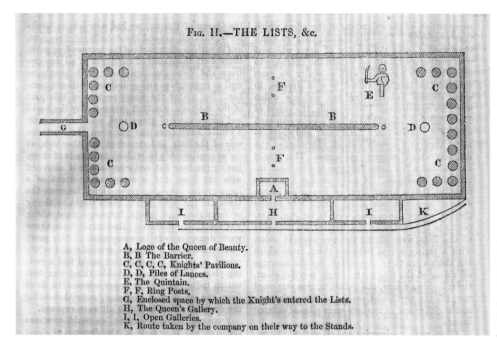

Fɪɢ. II.—THE LISTS, &c.

A, Loge of the Queen of Beauty.
B, B The Barrier.
C, C, C, C, Knights' Pavilions.
D, D, Piles of Lances.
E, The Quintain.
F, F, Ring Posts.
G, Enclosed space by which the Knight's entered the Lists.
H, The Queen's Gallery.
I, I, Open Galleries.
K, Route taken by the company on their way to the Stands.

Figure 7
Plan of the lists at Eglinton Castle, from Tait's Edinburgh Magazine (November 1839)
© Board of Trustees of the Armouries

The lists where the combats were to take place were constructed about a quarter of a mile to the northeast of the castle, on a piece of level ground about 700 feet long by 250 feet wide, down the centre length of which was erected a tilt barrier about 330 feet long. At either end of the lists were 21 tents, coloured in accordance with the armorial bearings of the knights who were to occupy them. On the north side of the lists the ground rose gently, forming a natural viewing area, and on the south side was erected a covered grandstand for the official guests, flanked by two open stands for other spectators. On the opposite side from the grandstand was another open stand for the gentlemen of the press and the artists sent to cover the event.

The route from the castle to the lists was by a winding path just over a mile long, and to convey his guests over the river, Eglinton had built an ornamental 'tournament bridge' cast in iron and decorated in the gothic style (the restored bridge still crosses the river Lugton today).

The official guests were beginning to arrive, and tents had been erected on the south lawn for those who could not be accommodated in the castle. The arrival of Lord Glenlyon and his Athol Highlanders excited particular attention:

'Lord Glenlyon and his band, completely equipped in full costume, with dirk and target and claymore, each man like his neighbour, accoutred and ready for actual service; his knapsack on his back, the word Athol thereon written, and each target with a dagger blade fixed and protruding from its centre'.[15]

Wednesday, 28 August - First Day of the Tournament
On the day of the tournament there were problems getting the thousands of visitors to the site. Some spectators made the journey to Kilwinning by train on the Glasgow and Ayrshire Railway, although there were complaints that the ticket prices had been trebled especially for the occasion. The special trains laid on for the tournament were drawn by the locomotive *Marmion*, appropriately named after another novel by Walter Scott. Some spectators converged on the two small towns of Irvine and Kilwinning only to find that the roads castle were gridlocked. There was a *'stream of pedestrians, in every variety of dress'* and *'carriages innumerable were hurrying on the scene of action, filled with ladies and gentlemen in fancy dresses - while cars, stage-coaches, and every other description of vehicle that could be pressed into service, were conveying their quotas of visitors'.*[16] Some spectators chose to come down the river Clyde from Glasgow and Paisley by steamer. Others came from even further afield, in ships from Liverpool, Belfast and Dublin. Estimates for the total number of visitors vary from between 40,000 to 80,000, and some sources put the figure as high as 100,000.

The crowd had been encouraged to dress for the occasion, and many did. On the north side of the lists, where the ordinary spectators gathered, *'Scotch plaids and bonnets were almost universal'.*[17] In the two open stands the spectators were *'arrayed in the gayest and most brilliant attire, intermixed with the most becoming costumes that could be selected from foreign nations and former generations.*[18] But this was nothing compared to the splendour of Eglinton's official guests. *'The grand stand, of course, was even doubly magnificent, and filled with spectators in every variety of costume, "all clinquant, all in gold". The ladies, radient with smiles and beauty, and sparkling with jewels, and their cavaliers, in equally gorgeous train, "every one that sat shewing like a mine"'.*[19] Finally, infront of the grandstand, in the space reserved for them, were the farmers and tenants of the Eglinton estate, also in costume *'with their blue bonnets and scarfs, and coats of antique cut'.* [20]

During the morning, as the crowd continued to grow, they were entertained by the Regimental Band of the 78th Highlanders, which had come over from Edinburgh especially for the occasion. By twelve o'clock most of the spectators had arrived, and were waiting patiently for the tournament to begin. It was then that *'the heavens, which had been gradually becoming more overclouded, suddenly began to pour down mischief on all this splendour'.*[21] The effect was dramatic. *'In the place where a few minutes before the whole glittered with drapery of all the colours of the rainbow, there was now presented nothing but one dull, unvarying scene of silk and cotton umbrellas'.*[22]

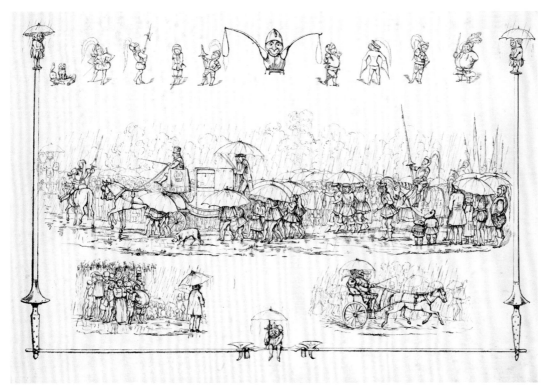

Figure 8
Cartoon showing procession to the lists, from The tournament, or, The days of chivalry reviv'd by R Doyle (London, ca. 1839) © *Board of Trustees of the Armouries*

At the castle, preparations had been underway for the procession to the lists, but this was now delayed because of the weather. At about one o'clock it stopped raining, but there was still no procession. Without the benefit of a dress rehearsal, it took Sir Charles Lamb, the Knight Marshal, and Lord Saltoun, the Judge of the Lists, much longer than expected to organise the participants, particularly as the Queen of Beauty, and the other lady visitors had decided to travel to the lists by covered coach because of the appalling weather. Not surprisingly, most of the eyewitnesses who left accounts can not confirm either the order of the procession, or who took part in it, and as a result tend to reprint the order that was listed in the official programme.

By two-thirty it was raining again, worse than before, and the spectators began to speculate that the tournament would be cancelled. But then, *'in the vicinity of the Castle, was to be distinguished something like a movement amongst the crowd of cavaliers; and by and bye, the headmost files turned into the course'.*[23] The patience of the crowd was finally rewarded, and even without the Queen of Beauty and the other ladies, the procession was an impressive site. *'The Knights, in their velvet hoods, and their steeds barbed with frontlet of steel, their helmets borne by their different esquires, themselves like pillars of iron as they rode, and than whom, in their perfect harness of proof, nothing could look more noble and imposing'.*[24] On reaching the lists the knights paid homage to the Queen of Beauty, who had already arrived by coach, and then retired to their tents to prepare themselves for the jousts. There were twelve competitors in all.

Archibald William Montgomerie, 13th Earl of Eglinton - Lord of the Tournament
William, 2nd Earl of Craven - Knight of the Griffin
Henry de la Poer Berseford, 3rd Marquis of Waterford - Knight of the Dragon
John Hume, Viscount Alford - Knight of the Black Lion
George Augustus Frederick John, 2nd Lord Glenlyon - Knight of the Gael
Archibald, Earl of Cassilis - Knight of the Dolphin
Hon. Captain Henry Edward Hall Gage - Knight of the Ram
Mr Walter Little Gilmour - Black Knight
Hon. Edward Stafford-Jerningham - Knight of the Swan
Capt. James Ogilvy Fairlie - Knight of the Golden Lion
Charles James Savile Montgomerie Lamb, Esq. - Knight of the White Rose
Sir Francis Hopkins, 2nd Baronet of Athboy - Knight of the Burning Tower
R J Lechmere, Esq. - Knight of the Red Rose

Walter Little Gilmour was a late replacement for John Campbell, who had not recovered from the injury he had received during the practices in London. Another contestant to scratch was Captain Maynard, who was ill. Other names appear in some of the accounts but were not present, including Lord Cranstoun (Knight of the Crane), Sir F Johnstone (the Knight of the Border), Captain Beresford (Knight of the Stag's Head) and Cecil Boothby (Knight of the Lion's Paw) who had all dropped out. Those who participated were all friends that Eglinton had known from different circumstances and different milieu. Some were family, other were neighbours with estates in Ayrshire, some were old school friends, and others acquaintances he had met through horse racing, hunting and various other sporting events. With the exception of Lechmere, they were all young men, aged from 23 years old to 35 years old, and in the prime of life.

The other major participants in the tournament were:

Jane Georgiana Sheridan, Lady Seymour - Queen of Beauty
Charles William Vane, 3rd Marquis of Londonderry - King of the Tournament
Alexander George Fraser, Lord Saltoun - Judge of Peace
Sir Charles Lamb - Knight Marshal

The first competition was to be a form of jousting known as tilting. The Joust was the most well known of tournament sports. It was a single combat between two mounted knights, each armed with a lance. In tilting the two knights jousted over a barrier or tilt with the aim of breaking their lances on their opponent. At the Eglinton Tournament, each contest would consist of three courses, and, probably for reasons of safety, the aim was to break the lance on the shoulder shield, and not on the helmet, which was actually the primary target in the Middle Ages.

With the day drawing on, and the rain still falling it was decided to dispense with much of the remaining pageantry *and the preparations for the commencement of the tilting were hurried through as speedily as possible - the knights, esquires, pages, and others, gallantly bearing up under the pelting of the rain, which, at this time, fell in torrents*.[25] At last the Marshal of the Lists gave the signal, there was fanfare of trumpets, and the Herald of the Tournament announced the rules of combat. These appear to have been drawn from the rules produced in the last years of the reign of Elizabeth I, written down by the Norroy King of Arms in 1602, which in turn were based on those composed by the Earl of Worcester in 1465.

Laws and Regulations for the Tournament
No Knight can be permitted to ride without having on the whole of his tilting pieces.
No Knight to ride more than six courses with the same opponent.
It is expressly enjoined by the Earl of Eglinton, and must be distinctly understood by each Knight upon engaging to run a course, that he is to strike his opponent on no other part than the shield, and that an *atteint* made elsewhere (or the lance broken across) will be adjudged foul, and advantages in former course forfeited.
Lances of equal length, substance, and quality, as far as can be seen, will be delivered to each Knight, and none others will be allowed.

NB: In default of the lances being splintered in any course, the judge will decide for the *attaint* made nearest to the centre of the shield.

Actions worthy of Honour
To break the most lances
To break the lance in more places than one
Not to put the lance in rest until near your opponent
To meet point to point of the lances
To strike on the emblazonment of shield
To perform all the determined course

Actions worthy of Dishonour
To break the lance across the opponent
To strike or hurt the horse
To strike the saddle
To drop the lance or sword
To lose the management of the horse at the encounter
To be unhorsed – the greatest dishonour
All lances broken by striking below the girdle to be disallowed

Actions most Worthy
To break the lance in many places

At the Tourney or Barrier
Two blows to be given in passing, and ten at the encounter.

THE JOUSTS

Regrettably the jousting cheque, the traditional method of scoring, appears not to have been used at the Eglinton Tournament, and the eye witness accounts of the combat vary. Aikman, Bulkeley, Curling and Richardson generally agree on the participants if not the details of each course. The discrepancies probably result from *'the narrators being at different points of the ground, and from the great rapidity with which the encounters of the knights took place'*.[26] The following is a reconstruction of events.

Jerningham vs Fairlie
First course: miss
Second course: miss
Third course: void as Jerningham's horse shied away from the tilt
Fourth course: unclear, but Bulkeley noted that *'the lance of the Golden Lion shivered on his antagonist's shield'*[27] and this is supported by Richardson's account
Jerningham was declared the victor

The most highly anticipated contest appears to have been between the host, the Earl of Eglinton, and the much admired Marquis of Waterford.

[Lord Eglinton] *'was clad in complete suit of richly gilded armour, which far outshone in brilliancy the panoply of his compeers. His noble mien and magnificent appearance, the beauty of his charger, and his skill in the management of the animal, drew down the repeated acclamations of the multitude. Nor was his opponent, the Knight of the Dragon, the Marquess of Waterford, observed with less interest by those who could identify him by his device'.*[28]

Eglinton vs Waterford
First course: unclear. Bulkeley and Richardson believed that Eglinton had broken his lance on his opponent's shield
Second course: void
Third course: All agree that Eglinton's lance struck home. Curling wrote that *'they met firmly at the centre of the barrier, with a vehemence that twisted the Knight of the Dragon almost round in his seat'*[29]
Eglinton was declared the victor.

The third course, between Sir Francis Hopkins and R J Lechmere *'was the most gallant-contested tilt of the day.'*[30]

Hopkins vs Lechmere
First course: unclear. Aikman and Richardson believed that only Hopkins lance had broken; Bulkeley saw both lances break

Figure 9
Engraving showing the joust between the Earl of Eglinton and the Marquis of Waterford, after J. H. Nixon, from The Eglinton Tournament by J. Richardson (London, 1843)

Second course: both lances broke. Aikman believed that during the second course Hopkins had delivered a foul blow to his opponent's head.

Third course: Hopkins broke his lance *'But wherefore droops the lance of the gallant Red Rose Knight? The spear of the Knight of the Burning Tower again shivers on his buckler. Not till unarming is it discovered that from the severity of the shock in the second joust, the Knight of the Red Rose had received a wound to his hand, which disabled him from bringing his lance to bear.'*[31] Richardson believed that is was during this course that Hopkins delivered a fowl blow to his opponent's head.

Hopkins was declared the victor.

In the procession Lord Glenlyon had *'aroused the pride of every Scotchman present, and rendered it a point of national interest that victory should float over his plumes.'*[32] When he appeared in the lists his Athol Highlanders prepared to roar him on to victory. *'The numerous band of hardy Highlanders, the followers of the Knight of the Gael could with difficulty be restrained in their allotted places, such was their anxiety for the success of their chieftain'.*[33]

Glenlyon vs Alford

First course: miss

Second course: miss

Third course: Bulkeley and Richardson both agree that Alford's lance broke. Bulkeley added that *'The lance of the Knight of the Gael strikes the helmet of his antagonist, carrying away his frowning crest, his gallant plume, and the silken gold-worked favour wrought by beauty's hand'*[34]

Alford was declared the victor

The result was not to the liking of Glenlyon's followers, and *'deep and frequent were their murmurs when the Knight of the Black Lion was proclaimed the victor.'*[35]

Following the fourth course there was a brief interlude, when a foot combat took place infront of the grandstand, between the jester, a professional actor by the name of Robert McIan, and Redbury (or Redburn) of the Life Guards. The two men armed with two-handed swords exchanged lusty blows until McIan's sword was broken in two and the contest was ended.

Figure 10
Cartoon showing the foot combat between McIan and Redbury, from The tournament, or, The days of chivalry reviv'd by R Doyle (London, ca. 1839)
© *Board of Trustees of the Armouries*

Waterford vs Alford

First course: miss

Second course: unclear. Bulkeley and Richardson believed that Alford broke the tip of his lance; but Aikman held that Waterford broke his lance

Third course: Most sources agree that Waterford broke his lance. Aikman wrote that *'the Marquis shivered his lance against the armour of his antagonist, on one occasion causing the broken portion to fly nearly 100 feet in the air.'*[36]

Waterford was declared the victor

That there were a large number of misses or crossed lances during the five courses was hardly surprising. The knights were inexperienced, despite the practices held in London, and the conditions were atrocious. All this time the rain had continued to fall, and the roof of the grandstand finally gave way under the weight of water, drenching its occupants. The temporary pavilion, where Eglinton had planned to entertain his official guests that night faired no better:

'an ill-fated messenger, with blanched cheek, bears to the Lord of the Tournament the sad announcement. The splendid banquet munificent hospitality had prepared for five hundred; the ball whereat a thousand, excited by delicious sounds, were to have moved in graceful dance; the elaborate preparations for the costly supper; - all, all, were destroyed by the envious flood'.[37]

Reluctantly Eglinton announced the suspension of the tournament until the following day (weather permitting) and the cancellation of the night's festivities. The procession then reformed and returned to the castle, where Eglinton arranged to give a small dinner for about two hundred guests. The ordinary spectators were now faced with the difficulties of travelling back to their homes or rented accommodation. The rain had turned the roads to quagmires, and they were jammed with carriages. Despite the special trains put on for the occasion, the Glasgow and Ayrshire Railway could not cope with the numbers of passengers. *'The station at Irvine was speedily blockaded by hundreds; the eagerness formerly spread over the whole extent of road became more intense as it was cooped up within the narrow space infront of the station-house; the struggle for precedence became alarming; and many retired from the crowd, preferring rather to wait for a later train than to enjure the jostling, the pushing and the other inconveniences'.*[38] The last train did not pull out of the station until after midnight.

Thursday, 29 August - Second Day of the Tournament
It rained for most of the day and there was no possibility of continuing the tournament, although the skies did clear around noon and by two o'clock there were many hopeful spectators in the stands. Eglinton announced that the day's events were cancelled and that the tournament would continue the next day at one o'clock. Nevertheless, for the visitors there was still much to see and enjoy: the band of the 78th Highlanders played on the front lawn of the castle; the Athol Highlanders drilled for several hours and played their bagpipes, watched by the Queen of Beauty; and in the lists two knights, Waterford and Alford, practiced running at the quintain (hitting a rotating dummy with a lance). In addition, inside the temporary pavilion (the roof having now been secured by new coverings), the armour that the contestants had worn on the previous day was laid out on three tables:

'showing evident marks of the rough usage it had received in the lists, and having lost its silvery polish from exposure to the storm. The armour here exhibited was of no tinsel fabrication, but had braced the persons of knights in the former days of the Tournament: it had been collected from all parts of Britain and of Europe.'[39]

A number of impromptu events were laid on to entertain the official guests staying in the castle. The first was a foot-combat with broadswords between Prince Louis Napoleon and Charles Lamb, which lasted for the best part of an hour. The contest was frequently interrupted to enable the participants to raise their visors and take a breather. *'The faces of the combatants, accordingly, when their visors were torn open to relieve them were damp and death-like with exhaustion and the violence of their exertions.'*[40] In the end, Lamb was considered to have had the best of it, but no victor was declared, possibly out of respect for the Prince.

A second foot combat between the Hon. F Carteris and Count Valentine Esterhazy, turned into a comical tourney or melee between two teams of knights. They replaced their helmet crests with apples and oranges respectively, and armed themselves with mops and brooms that one of the guests had found. As mops and brooms came together, apples and oranges flew in all directions. Helmets ran with juice and it was impossible to *'distinguish which was which, or a Knight of the Orange from the bearer of the Apple. The arena was filled with splinters and fragments of the staves, and the air with the smashed pieces of fruit from their crests'.*[41] During the tourney Lord Craven was injured in the face, but not so seriously as to deter him from jousting the next day. One of the other guests, Count Persigny, then demonstrated the lance exercise, before Count Harrack and Mr. Chartres *'engaged with skill and ardour in a match at singlesticks'.*[42]

Although the temporary pavilion had been aired throughout the day, the banquet and ball were postponed once more. Eglinton gave an elegant dinner to one hundred and fifty guests in the upper drawing room of the castle, followed by a ball, which continued into the early hours of the morning.

Friday, 30 August - Third Day of the Tournament

Figure 11
Engraving of the Lists at Eglinton Castle, after Edward Corbould, from The Eglinton Tournament by 'B' (London, 1843) © *Board of Trustees of the Armouries*

The weather finally relented and the day was one of brilliant sunshine. Despite the short notice, the Glasgow and Ayrshire Railway had managed to lay on additional services, and as there were not as many spectators as on the Wednesday (perhaps several thousand less) there was less strain on the local transport system. Most of the crowd arrived between two and three o'clock and as before, they waited patiently for the tournament to begin. This time the procession to the lists was as published in the official programme:

'*The Queen and her Court, mounted upon their plumed steeds, had this day their place in the Procession; and the Lady Archers also trooped along in full costume of their forest craft... The welkin rang with shouts and acclamations, as the fair faces of the ladies appeared amongst the glistening helmets, tall lances, and all the pride and circumstance of chivalry.*'[43]

The King of the Tournament and the Queen of Beauty then took their places, and there was a flourish of trumpets as the knights were summoned one-by-one to pay their *devours* to Lady Seymour. The knights then rode round the lists and received the favours of their ladies. When all was ready the Herald of the Tournament proclaimed the laws of the tournament, which was the signal for the jousting to begin.

There are more discrepancies in the published accounts as to who took part in the jousts on the third day, and the accounts themselves are less descriptive. The following appears to be a likely reconstruction of events.

The first joust was between Viscount Glenlyon and Viscount Alford.

Glenlyon vs Alford

First course: *'Lord Glenlyon fairly and gallantly broke his spear'*[44]
Second course: miss
Third course: miss
Glenlyon was declared the victor

The next course was between Lord Craven and Captain Fairlie. The *'appearance of Earl Craven excited considerable interest, from the circumstance that the armour in which he was clad was that which was worn by his ancestor, then Baron Hilton, at the field of Cressy'*.[45]

Craven vs Fairlie

First course: *'The first shock between these knights was the finest passage of arms in the whole Tournament. Both knights met in full career; the lances of each was shivered; that of his Lordship being broken almost at the gauntlets grasp,*[46]
Second course: miss
Third course: Craven broke his lance
Craven was declared the victor

Lechmere vs Eglinton

First course: miss
Second course: miss
Third course: *'The Lord of the Tournament's lance... shattered with a thundering clash; it rent by the shock his antagonist's shield'*[47]
Eglinton was declared the victor

The identity of the participants in the fourth course is hotly disputed. Most sources, including probably the two most reliable (Aikman and Bulkeley) have the Marquis of Waterford jousting against Little Gilmour. Some give the two combatants as Viscount Alford and Lord Waterford, and others as Little Gilmour and Captain Beresford (who was not even present).

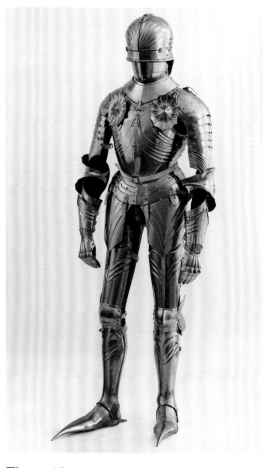

Figure 12
The armour of the Marquis of Waterford. European, 19th century. Royal Collection © HM Queen Elizabeth II

Waterford vs Little Gilmour
First course: miss
Second course: miss
Third course: both lances broke
Fourth course: miss
Undecided

All accounts agree that the next course was between the Earl of Cassilis and Charles Lamb, who were both making their first appearance in the lists.

Cassilis vs Lamb
First course: miss
Second course: miss
Third course: miss
Undecided

The next joust between the Hon. Mr Jerningham and the Hon. Captain Gage was similarly uneventful.

Jerningham vs Gage
First course: miss
Second course: miss
Third course: miss
Undecided

The final course was run between Captain J O Fairlie and Sir F Hopkins, both of whom had jousted on the Wednesday.

Fairlie vs Hopkins
First course: Aikman felt that the lances had slightly touched
Second course: *'the lance of Mr. Fairlie was shivered'* [44]
Third course: Once again Aikman felt that the lances had slightly touched
Fairlie was declared the victor

The jousting had not been as exciting as the first day of the tournament. And Bulkeley observed that:

'Be it that the ground, saturated with rain, was most heavy; towards the close of the jousts absolutely ploughed up; or that the horses, perhaps wanting exercise, were less steady, the tilting on this day was not considered so good as that on Wednesday. The exercise at St. Johns Tiltyard, however, no more gave evidence of the proficiency to which it was brought, than the baby of a month old exhibits the prowess of the man of five-and-thirty – the jousts were full of spirit, and of the highest interest'. [49]

Nevertheless, the crowd were enthralled. Curling admitted that *'had I but a steed and coat of mail at command, I could almost willingly have compounded for a broken limb, for the chance of one tilt at the shield of any of the knights there assembled'.* [50]

At the same time as the jousts were proceeding, there were a number of other sideshow events, including running at the ring (capturing a ring on the end of a lance) and running at the quintain. *'The quintain excited much amusement, since, if the Saracen were not struck so fair and full as to be knocked over, he riposted with a swinging blow from his ponderous sword'.* [51] These two latter events were in fact training exercises for squires and young knights, and not strictly speaking part of a tournament in the Middle Ages.

The final event of the day *'was considered the most animating and entertaining contest'.* [52] This was a tourney or melee. The tourney was the earliest form of tournament combat, and was a mock battle fought between two teams on horseback. In medieval tournaments the contestants fought with lances, and when these broke, with swords. There was also an amusing variation that used only blunt weapons with the aim of smashing or dislodging the opponents' helmet crests, hence the term *crest fallen*. At the Eglinton Tournament two teams were formed:

18

Scottish and Irish knights	English knights
Earl of Eglinton	Viscount Alford
Marquis of Waterford	R J Lechmere
W Little Gilmour	Charles Lamb
Lord Glenlyon	Hon. H Jerningham

The knights were armed with swords but were forbidden to thrust, because of the danger of serious injury, and permitted only to strike. Sir Charles Lamb, the Marshal of the Lists, was the judge who would decide when the combat was ended. The teams charged at each other from opposite ends of the lists and exchanged blows as they swept passed. The sword of Lord Glenlyon *'was bent round like a hoop with one blow'*.[53] One combat nearly resulted in serious consequences. Jerningham had his sword arm forced back by Little Gilmour, and as a result the point of his lance-rest *'penetrated between the gauntlet and the armour, among the veins and tendons of the wrist, severing some of them, and lacerating the arm'*.[54] He was quickly treated on the spot by one of the spectators, Dr Guthrie of Ayr. Waterford and Alford, having failed at the first pass to strike off the other's helmet crest, suddenly wheeled round to renew the combat without going back to their respective stations. They *'rode at each other with all the fury of the animals they wore in their crests, dealing each other blows as they passed'*.[55] The spectators were thoroughly enjoying the combat between the two when to their disappointment Sir Charles Lamb:

'seeing the rules had been broken, dashed between the combatants, and sadly deprived the spectators of a rich and skilful display of a single equestrian combat, but by doing so, perhaps, preserved one of the knights for days of future achievement; as it certainly appeared in this case that valour had got the better of discretion'.[56]

Figure 13
Engraving of the combat between the Marquis of Waterford and Viscount Alford, after Edward Corbould, from The Eglinton Tournament by 'B' (London, 1843) © *Board of Trustees of the Armouries*

The tourney concluded the events for the day and the Marshal of the Lists ordered the procession to reform and return to the castle. Eglinton, in his enthusiasm, declared that the tournament would continue the next day, but most of the spectators began to make their long journeys home. Curling described the difficulties many experienced:

'Accordingly, the flock of visitors in the different towns and hamlets fluctuated about for some time, with no means of escape. Coaches, cars, and busses were taken for days to come, and even post-horses … Unless, therefore, you took quarter-staff in hand, and your baggage on your back, it was necessary to bide your time, till the first rush had swept off.'[57]

The temporary pavilion having been repaired and the rooms thoroughly aired, Eglinton was finally able to deliver the grand entertainment that he had planned for his guests. Bulkeley was one of those who attended, and left a magnificent account of the celebrations. Eglinton led Lady Seymour down the grand staircase from the castle, which was lined on either side by retainers dressed as an *archer guard*, and into the reception room. The banners of the knights were hung from the walls, and at the far end of the room were the band of the 2nd Dragoon Guards. Bulkeley recorded the costumes of some of those present. Lady Seymour was dressed in:

'A superb antique brocade silk kirtle, raised with silver, gold and various colours; vest of white velvet, with demi sleeves of silver tissue damask wire; placard of gold, set with precious stones; skayne (or veil) of silver canvass, and chaplet of flowers'.[58]

And Eglinton wore:

'A rich knight's costume of the 15ᵗʰ century; a short tunic of dark-blue velvet, embroidered round the bottom with a motto, "Gardes bien," fleir-de-lis, and an amulet, in gold; the sleeves of rich cloth; white silk hose; ankle-boots of blue and yellow kid, braided with gold'.[59]

At ten o'clock guests followed the Lord of the Tournament and the Queen of Beauty into dinner. The banqueting hall was a splendid site:

'hung with trophies and gothic embellishments, presented an elevated table of honour surmounted by a dais; a gold service, and numerous cups, won by the race-horses bread by the Lord of the Tournament and his grandfather, adorned it. Three other tables, covered with a profusion of the richest plate, ran the whole length of the saloon'.[60]

Eglinton and Lady Seymour sat at the centre of the table of honour along with the Duke and Duchess of Montrose, the Marquis and Marchioness of Londonderry, and Prince Louis Napoleon. At one end of the table was the Marquis of Waterford and his retinue, and at the other Viscount Glenlyon and his followers. Behind each knight was a man-at-arms bearing his gonfalon (standard). In all there were between 400 and 500 guests. The meal did not disappoint the occasion.

'The repast, in grandeur and sumptuousness of design, in elegance and finish to the minutest detail, was perfection. The chef of the Lord of the Tournament ranks high in the gastronomic annals as a cordon-bleau; and the celebrated Mr. Thorton was assisted by several London cooks of eminence… Mr Chinery purveyed the rich wine that flowed in copious libations'.[61]

Figure 14
Engraving of the Ball, after J H Nixon, from The Eglinton Tournament by J Richardson (London, 1843)
© *Board of Trustees of the Armouries*

The Earl of Eglinton proposed the health of Lady Seymour, and the Marquis of Londonderry returned thanks on behalf of the Queen of Beauty. Eglinton then proposed several other toasts, including one to Lord Glenlyon, thanking him for the great part he had played, and for bringing his Athol Highlanders to the tournament. The Marquis of Waterford then proposed a toast to the Lord of the Tournament, *'Had there been no Eglinton, there had been no Tournament'*,[62] which was followed by a spontaneous round of applause. The ladies then retired.

At midnight the party adjourned to the castle until the ballroom was made ready. The ballroom was also sumptuously decorated *'at the upper end of which was a throned canopy, fringed with gold and silver, surmounted with plumes, and lined at the back with the cloth of gold used at the coronation of England's queen'.*[63] In addition, *'the room was illuminated by no less than 30 wax candles, supported by ormolu antique bronzes, around the walls; while from the roof hung ten or twelve gorgeous candelabra, thickly studded with wax lights.*[64] Even the floor was set *'in beautiful devices with the arms of Eglinton'.*[65] At two o'clock in the morning there was a light supper, and the ball finally ended at about five o'clock.

The following day was one of incessant rain, and no further competition was possible. One-by-one Eglinton's guests began to take their leave, and the great tournament was over.

Success or Failure

Opinions on the success or otherwise of the Eglinton Tournament varied as one might expect. The press reports, almost without exception, were dominated by the rain-soaked first day, and the tournament was later parodied extensively both in print and on the London stage. Eglinton's friends, however, certainly had no doubts as to the success of the event, and two hundred and thirty nine of them subscribed to a trophy at no less then 20 guineas apiece to express their thanks and admiration. There was also a tangible economic benefit to the local community. Bulkeley reported that an estimated *'500,000l were expended in the neighbourhood by the visitors and strangers'*[66] and even allowing for some slight exaggeration, it is not surprising that a month after the event the residents of Irvine gave a banquet in Eglinton's honour.

Figure 15
Engraving of the Eglinton Testimonial, from the Illustrated London News
© Board of Trustees of the Armouries

Of the two men most closely associated with the tournament, Eglinton himself never sought to repeat the experiment. The cost of the event was something in the region of £30,000 or £40,000, most of which went to Samuel Pratt. Pratt must have made a tidy profit from the event, especially as he seems to have neglected to pay some of his bills. The following February he opened a new exhibition at Grosvenor Street to display the armours worn by the knights at the tournament, and when this had run its course, *'the long-announced sale of the magnificent armour, appointments, and paraphernalia used at the Eglintoun tournament commenced at Messrs. Oxenham's room.'*[67] But in the end Pratt too must have been disappointed. The prices realised at the sale were not as high as he hoped. Hopkins' armour was sold for only 35 guineas, Jerningham's for only £36, and Lamb's for only 24 guineas. The throne of the Queen of Beauty even had to be withdrawn when it failed to reach its reserve.

Of the independent witnesses, the romantics like Curling, whose expectations of the event had been so high, felt that:

'When you looked upon the scene as now enacted, and remembered with difficulty that you lived in the dull mechanical money-getting, common-place year of eighteen hundred and thirty-nine, in place of some four hundred years agone "in the dark backward and abysm of time", you felt that, as nothing but a dream of the past ever came up to what you then was mixed up in; so was it proportionably unlikely you could ever again behold so perfectly delightful a spectacle.'[68]

Others like Aikman were more critical. He felt that *'the tilting was allowed on all sides not to be so interesting as was anticipated'* and believed that the cause of this disappointment was *'the fact, that there was all the appearance of danger, while there was none in reality'.*[69] The crowd had expected horses to recoil from the encounters, and knights to be unhorsed, but none of this happened. Without danger *'the interest of the spectators sensibly diminished'* and because each course was more or less the same as the other this *'tended partly to increase the general apathy'.*[70]

As an accurate representation of a medieval or even an Elizabethan tournament it was a failure. Except for the tilting, most of the forms of combat including the running at the ring and quintain and the crest-smashing melee more properly belonged to the 17th century carousel which was designed chiefly as a display of horsemanship. But then, it was never intended to be accurate. Eglinton knew this:

'I am aware of the manifold deficiencies in its exhibition – more perhaps than those who were not so deeply interested in it; I am aware that it was a very humble imitation of the scenes which my imagination had portrayed, but I have, at least, done something towards the revival of chivalry ... I have, I believe been censured for the waste of money, which might have been better bestowed upon religious or charitable purposes. I humbly conceive that I could not have more profitably employed it than in providing an innocent and interesting amusement ... I cannot hope that this attempt of mine will be followed'.[71]

The tournament was attempting to be a living re-enactment of the literary romances. In fact those who defended it likened it to the Passage of Arms at Ashby de la Zouche and above all applauded its spectacle. They agreed that despite its failings and the weather, the tournament had been a magical moment. Even Aikman was forced to agree:

'Whatever opinion may be formed of the success of the Tournament, as an imitation of ancient manners and customs, we heard only one feeling of admiration expressed at the gorgeousness of the whole scene, considered only as a pageant. Even on Wednesday, when the procession was seen to the greatest possible disadvantage, the dullest eye glistened with delight as the lengthy and stately train swept slow into the marshalled lists'.[72]

A REVIEW OF THE EGLINTON TOURNAMENT OF 1839

Text by the Reverend John Richardson
Illustrations by James Henry Nixon
Lithographed by Aubrey and Loiellot
Published by Colnaghi and Puckle, London 1843

This work describes itself as a *'series of views'* representing the Eglinton Tournament from drawings made *'on the spot expressly for this work'*. Although there is an introduction and each picture is accompanied by text, it was intended to be a collection of illustrations, rather than a blow-by-blow account of the tournament. The book presented what it considered to be the epitomic events in a series of twenty one plates: the procession to the lists, a general view of the lists, the challenge, the joust, the mêlée, the presentation of the knights, the banquet, and the ball. The procession to the lists evolves over fourteen plates and the other events have a single plate each.

The publishers were Colnaghi and Puckle of 14 Pall Mall East in London, who were print dealers with an international reputation. However, who commissioned the work is a matter for some debate. Dominic Paul Colnaghi was a collector of armour, and was the original possessor of a large part of the Meyrick Collection. As such he may have had a personal interest in the Eglinton Tournament, and decided to publish the book. Alternatively, Samuel Pratt, who would have known Colnaghi as a fellow art dealer and a collector of armour, may have suggested it to him. Pratt, as the organiser of the tournament, may even have commissioned the book himself, and there is some evidence in the composition of the illustrations to suggest that Eglinton himself may have had a strong influence on the final work.

The introduction and the accompanying text were written by the Reverend John Richardson. Richardson was a minor literary figure. He was educated at Eton and Trinity Hall, Cambridge, and graduated as a Bachelor of Laws (LL.B) in 1816. He was a student at Lincoln's Inn, and a special pleader in the Inner Temple, before deciding to take holy orders. From about 1832 he was connected with the popular press, and appears to have covered the Eglinton Tournament for *The Times*.

The original drawings from which the plates were engraved were made by the artist James Henry Nixon (sometimes referred to as John Henry Nixon). Nixon was a professional glass painter, who in 1828 had gone into business with John Hancock, one of the first manufacturers of enamel and glass colours. He then left the firm of Hancock, Nixon and Hunt, and went into partnership with John Hedgeland. Hedgeland was inspired by early Renaissance glass, but as the influence of Pugin and the Medievalists became stronger, this became unfashionable. Nixon left, and in 1836 set up the firm of Ward & Nixon (London) with Thomas Ward, a well-known lead glazier. The business prospered, and over the next twenty years they produced windows that were shipped all over the world. In 1844 Nixon submitted designs for the new windows in the House of Lords, but failed to get the commission. Nixon's work as a glass painter may well have brought him into contact with Samuel Pratt.

Nixon appears to have been a pupil of John Martin, a well known painter of historical subjects, and in 1830 he exhibited an oil on canvas entitled *Macbeth, Act IV, scene 1* at the Royal Academy. It drew favourable reviews: *'We have seen nothing to approach so entirely to the Martin-like character of composition, imagination and sublimity'*.[73] Other works followed, including *'the Tempest'* and *'Richard's dream'* (Richard III). In 1834 he contributed to *'Illustrations; landscape, historical, and antiquarian, to the poetical works of Sir Walter Scott, bart.'* compiled by John Martin. Nixon was developing a reputation as a painter of genre, historical and scriptural subjects, and as an artist he may well have been known to Colnaghi.

In 1837 Nixon exhibited another oil on canvas at the Royal Academy entitled *'Chess - Louis XIV and Cardinal de Retz with the principal nobility of the Court'* and the following year another work, *'Queen Victoria's Progress to Guildhall on 9th November 1837'*. It was probably this latter painting, which was on show at the Royal Academy in the year that the Eglinton Tournament was announced, that won for the Nixon the commission to produce the original illustrations for this work.

The book does not follow the chronological development of the tournament, but it leads the reader to assume that all of the events illustrated took place on the same day. This is not the case. The tournament actually took place over three days with combats on both 28 and 30 August. There were, however, significant differences between the events as they unfurled over the two days. A study of contemporary written accounts of the tournament reveal that the majority of the incidents portrayed actually took place on 30 August. On 28 August there was heavy rain, and neither the Queen of Beauty nor the lady visitors took part in the procession to the lists, and the grand banquet and ball planned for that night were cancelled. All of these events took place on 30 August. Only two plates actually show events that happened on the 28 August: plates sixteen and seventeen which depict the Challenge, and the Joust between the Earl of Eglinton and the Marquis of Waterford.

Figure 16
Queen Victoria's Progress to Guildhall, 1838, by James Henry Nixon.
© *Guildhall Art Gallery, City of London/Bridgeman Art Library*

There are also some errors and discrepancies in the accompanying text. Richardson repeats a mistake common to all of the published accounts of the tournament, reprinting the order of the procession to the lists from the official programme, which was produced well in advance of the event. However, some of the knights who had intended to take part were not present. There was no Knight of the Crane (Lord Cranstoun), Knight of the Stag's Head (Captain Beresford), Knight of the Border (Sir F. Johnstone) or Knight of the Lion's Paw (Cecil Boothby). The Black Knight was due to be John Campbell but he had not recovered from an injury received during the practices at the Eyre Arms near Regents Park, and was replaced by W. Little Gilmour.

Richardson also gives an incomplete description of the jousting in the text accompanying plate seventeen. He gives a personal account of the tilting on the first day, but not of the tilting on the third day. To cover this gap he actually reprints another newspaper report of the jousting for both days. There is a possible explanation for this discrepancy. Although Richardson was present at the tournament on the first day, it is unclear whether he remained until the third day, as no report of the events of the 30 August was subsequently published in *The Times*. Richardson may not have been present on this day, and his account, therefore, is highly suspect. He could easily have written the text based on others already published. For example, both Aikman and Bulkeley had described the costumes worn by some of the guests at the banquet and ball, and these are reprinted in Richardson's account.

Figure 17
Engraving of the Earl of Eglinton crossing the Tournament Bridge, after Edward Corbould, from The Eglinton Tournament by 'B' (London, 1843) © *Board of Trustees of the Armouries*

The value of this book, however, lies with the illustrations and not the text. They are beautifully and subtly executed by the artist in the Romantic style, and are highly evocative of the Victorian image of the Middle Ages. Nixon shows the procession to the lists as it took place on 30 August when it was complete in all its parts. He includes the Queen of Beauty and the lady visitors and their attendants, and excludes the knights who were in the official programme, but did not take part. The route of the cavalcade was about a mile long, and from the castle it followed the left bank of the river Lugton in a sweeping curve until it reached a bridge. This bridge was a magnificent example of the Gothic Revival built especially for the tournament. Most artists who captured the scene made a point of showing the bridge, and the procession passing across it. On the other side of the bridge the procession continued along the right bank of the river. Along the whole of the processional route was a barrier behind which the spectators stood. Nixon does not show either the bridge or any spectators. If, as is claimed, the plates were taken from drawings made in situ then, from the position of the castle and assuming that he did not move, Nixon appears therefore to have been seated on the lawn in the park. Although there are few other indications, the absence of spectators and a representation of the tournament bridge may confirm this position.

The composition of some of the illustrations is interesting. Lady Montgomerie, the most prominent of the Lady Visitors and Eglinton's mother, is shown accompanied by his stepfather Sir Charles Lamb (the Knight Marshal of the Lists). The Marques of Londonderry (the King of the Tournament), Lady Seymour (the Queen of Beauty) and the Earl of Eglinton (Lord of the Tournament) all have a plate in their own right, as befits their importance. The other knights either share or have individual plates, and there appears at first glance to be no order of precedence. The Marquis of Waterford (the Knight of the Dragon) shares a plate with the Earl of Craven (the Knight of the Griffin), and his retinue spills over onto the next plate – with Viscount Alford (the Knight of the Black Lion). Waterford was, after Eglinton, the most successful combatant at the tournament, and would seem to deserve a plate in his own right. Lord Glenlyon (the Knight of the Gael) whose Highlanders played such a prominent part in the event, does have his own plate, as does Captain James Ogilvie Fairlie (the Knight of the Golden Lion), perhaps because they were fellow Scots, and in Fairlie's case because he was a close friend and neighbour of Eglinton's. The other single plate is occupied by Charles Lamb (the Knight of the White Rose) who was Eglinton's half brother. This would almost suggest that Nixon was influenced in his choice and treatment of some of the participants.

Figure 18
Engraving of the Queen of Beauty, after J H Nixon, from The Eglinton Tournament by J Richardson (London, 1843) © Board of Trustees of the Armouries

After the general view of the lists, Eglinton becomes, not unexpectedly, the most prominent figure in the remaining plates. His combat with the Marquis of Waterford is made the subject of the Challenge and the Joust, and he is shown engaged against the Hon. Edward Stafford-Jerningham (the Knight of the Swan) in the melee. At the conclusion of the tournament, Eglinton is then illustrated receiving the wreath of victory from Lady Seymour, and finally, after the banquet scene, he is shown again, with Lady Seymour, presiding over the Ball.

Although Colnaghi and Puckle had confirmed their intention to publish the work within days of the end of the tournament, it took four years to produce. A number of rivals had already published illustrated volumes by then, but the scale of Colnaghi's work outdid them all. There were three different printings: with black and white illustrations (for 5 guineas); with tinted illustrations (for 6 guineas); and a large folio in full colour with a highly illuminated letter press (for 10 guineas). The latter printing of *The Eglinton Tournament* is the most prized of Colnaghi's collections from this period, and the subject of this facsimile reprint. In the words of the review published in *The Mirror*:

'This work must be seen to be properly appreciated'

NOTES

[1] Richardson 1843: 2
[2] *The Times*, 16 April 1838
[3] Anon 1840: 3-4
[4] Anon 1840: 15-16
[5] Richardson 1843: 1
[6] The Times, 15 July, 1839: 5
[7] The Times, 5 August, 1839: 3
[8] Curling 1839: 4
[9] Curling 1839: 9
[10] Curling 1839: 10-11
[11] *Glasgow Constitutional*, reprinted in *The Times*, 29 August, 1839: 3
[12] Curling 1839: 15
[13] Bulkeley 1840: 6
[14] Aikman 1839: 6
[15] Curling 1839: 16
[16] Aikman 1839: 7
[17] Aikman 1839: 7
[18] Aikman 1839: 7
[19] Curling 1839: 23
[20] Curling 1839: 23
[21] Curling 1839: 23
[22] Aikman 1839: 9
[23] Curling 1839: 24
[24] Curling 1839: 24
[25] Aikman 1839: 10
[26] Richardson 1843: description to plate xvii
[27] Bulkeley 1840: 41
[28] Richardson 1843: description to plate xvii
[29] Curling 1839: 30
[30] Aikman 1839: 12
[31] Bulkeley 1840: 44
[32] Aikman 1839: 12
[33] Anon 1840: 33-34
[34] Bulkeley 1840: 45
[35] Anon 1840: 34
[36] Aikman 1839: 12

[37] Bulkeley 1840: 48-49
[38] Aikman 1839: 13
[39] Anon 1840: 39-40
[40] Curling 1839: 37
[41] Curling 1839: 38-39
[42] Bulkeley 1840: 63
[43] Curling 1839: 40-41
[44] Aikman 1839: 14
[45] Aikman 1839: 14
[46] Aikman 1839: 14
[47] Bulkeley 1840: 73
[48] Aikman 1839: 15
[49] Bulkeley 1840: 73
[50] Curling 1839: 45
[51] Bulkeley 1840: 76
[52] Aikman 1839: 15
[53] Curling 1839: 47
[54] Anon 1840: 51
[55] Curling 1839: 47
[56] Anon 1840: 51-52
[57] Curling 1839: 48
[58] Bulkeley 1840: 115
[59] Bulkeley 1840: 125
[60] Bulkeley 1840: 80
[61] Bulkeley 1840: 81-82
[62] Bulkeley 1840: 87
[63] Anon 1840: 55
[64] Aikman 1839: 15-16
[65] Bulkeley 1840: 90
[66] Bulkeley 1840: 96
[67] The Times, 18 July, 1840, p. 6
[68] Curling 1839: 45
[69] Aikman 1839: 16
[70] Aikman 1839: 16
[71] Richardson 1843: 2
[72] Aikman 1839: 16
[73] Literary Gazette, 1831: 90

BIBLIOGRAPHY

Aikman, J 1839 *An account of the tournament at Eglinton : revised and corrected by several of the knights* (illustrations by W Gordon). Edinburgh

Anon, 1840 *The passage of arms at Eglinton, 28 August 1839.* London

Anon. 1839 *The tournment: a mock-heroic ballad.* London (illustrated by Alfred Crowquill)

Anstruther, 1963 *The knight and the umbrella: an account of the Eglinton Tournament 1839.* London

'B', 1840 *The Eglinton tournament.* (illustrations by E Corbould). London

Buchan, P 1840 *The Eglinton tournament and gentleman unmasked.* London

Bulkeley, J 1840 *A right faithful chronique of the ladies and knights who gained worship at The Grand Tourney holden at his castle by the Earl of Eglintoun.* London

Carre, J B L 1795 Panoplie, 2 vols. *The Court Journal.* Chalons sur Marne and Paris: 1838-39

Coltman Clephan, R 1919 *The tournament, its periods and phases.* London

Cripps-Day, F H 1925 *A record of armour sales, 1891-1924.* London

Curling, H 1839 *The Field of the Cloth of Gold at Eglintoun.* London

Doyle, R 1839 The tournament or The days of chivalry reviv'd. London
The Gentleman's Magazine: 414-416

Girouard, M 1981 *The return to Camelot: Chivalry and the English gentleman.* London

Grose, F 1786 *A treatise on ancient armour and weapons.* London

Honour, H 1955 The Eglinton tournament. *Country Life* (20 October): 895-899

Honour, H 1979 *Romanticism.* London

Meyrick, S R 1824 A critical inquiry in ancient armour. *New Sporting Magazine*: 186-187

Pratt, S L 1838 *Catalogue of the exhibition of ancient arms and armour.* London

Reid, W 1991/92 'Such sights as youthful poets dream': the Earl of Eglinton's tournament and society. *Livrustkammaren: Journal of the Royal Armoury*: 104-128

Richardson, J 1843 *The Eglinton tournament: this series of views representing the tournament held at Eglinton Castle in the year 1839* (illustrations by J H Nixon). London

Tait's Edinburgh Magazine 1839: 697-716

Tolson, J 2008 The thirteenth Earl of Eglinton: a notable Scottish sportsman. *Sport in History*: 472-490

Trappes-Lomax, M 1936 The Eglinton tournament. *Country Life* (25 January: 96-98)

Watts, K 1989 150 years ago: the Eglinton tournament and the Gothic revival. *Park Lane Arms Fair*: 22-27

The
EGLINTON

TOVRNAMENT.

LONDON,
COLNACHI & PUCKLE.
1843.

To

The Right Honorable

Archibald William Montgomerie,

Earl of Eglinton and Winton,

Baron Ardrossan,

&c. &c. &c.

This Series of Views,

representing

The Tournament held at Eglinton Castle,

in the Year 1839,

From Drawings made on the spot expressly for this Work,

by

James Henry Nixon,

with

Historical and Descriptive Notices,

by

The Reverend John Richardson, L.L.B.

is respectfully dedicated,

by His Lordship's

most obliged and obedient Servant,

Edward Puckle.

(late Colnaghi & Puckle).

London, No. 23 Cockspur Street, Charing Cross,
1st Dec.r, 1843.

LIST OF PLATES.

DAY & HAGHE, LITH^{RS} TO THE QUEEN.
MDCCCXLIII.

THE EGLINTON TOURNAMENT.

INTRODUCTION.

" All furnish'd, all in arms,
　All plumed like estridges, that with the wind
　Bated like eagles, having lately bathed,
　Glittering in golden coats, like images;
　As full of spirit as the month of May,
　And gorgeous as the sun at Midsummer."
　　　　　　　　SHAKSPEARE, PART I., HENRY IV.

" Listen, lively lordlings all,
　Lithe and listen unto mee,
　And I will tell of a noble earle,
　　The noblest earle in the north countrie."
　　　　　　ANCIENT BALLAD, THE RISING IN THE NORTH.

" —— Stoden, the castell all aboutin
　Of all maner of mynstrales
　And jestours that tellen tales
　Both of wepyng and of game,
　And of all that longeth unto fame."
　　　　　　　　CHAUCER, 3RD BOKE OF FAME.

" With store of ladies, whose bright eyes
　Rain influence, and judge the prize."
　　　　　　　　L'ALLEGRO.

MONGST the long list of the Tournaments of ancient days, and the pageants of ancient and modern times, none has excited more curiosity than the Tournament which was held in the park of Eglinton Castle, in the month of August, 1839. And it may be added, no pageant more fully gratified the high expectations which had been raised. This celebrated revival of the splendid feats and glories of the ancestry of the nobles and gentles of the land—of the dames and damoiselles of days long gone by, may be regarded as a magnificent illustration of the history of ancient chivalry; as a living picture, on a grand and commensurate scale, of the warlike sports and pastimes of the great and good of the middle ages of England, and Scotland, and Ireland; as a moving and animated panorama of the habits and customs of those who, in times past, directed the energies of a great nation; a tableau, elucidating the modes and manners over which 300 years have thrown their shadow, and presenting at one view, to more than 100,000 spectators, a graphic and an intelligible exposition of one of the most important pages in the narrative of antiquity.

" —————— all of high degree
　Who knighthood loved and deeds of chivalry,
　Throng'd to the lists, and envy'd to behold
　The names of others, not their own, enroll'd."

To the Earl of Eglinton the public are indebted for this gorgeous spectacle; and the debt which is due to him from all admirers of the manly amusements and boundless hospitality of the knights and barons of old; from all who respect the valour and dignity of the aristocracy of Great Britain; from all who venerate the institutions which are the origin of the present intelligence and refinement of the general community; and from all to whom female loveliness and honour are interesting, is one which it will take long to repay, and which must be acknowledged with the most fervid devotion and thankfulness.

No sooner was it rumoured, during the season of 1839, that a " Tournament" was about to be got up, and that preparations were being made for the celebration of it on the domains of a " belted earl" in the Kingdom of Scotland, than all persons of good taste, and rank, and fashion were on the *qui vive*. Those who were in London in the spring of 1839 must well remember the " sensation" which the rumour of such a thing excited. Inquiries were being made everywhere, where intelligence could be gained, into the particulars of the reported fact, and, as soon as it was ascertained to be true, the most intense curiosity arose on all sides to be acquainted with the details.

The Earl of Eglinton, in order to carry out the views which he formed, and practically to illustrate the ideas he had conceived, from early reading and traditionary lore, of the real nature of a Tournament, resolved to spare no expense in the arrangements, but to have the whole conducted in a manner that should at once evince the correctness of his taste, the munificence of his hospitality, and the chivalric aspirations of his mind. The details of the preparations were confided to the Messrs. Pratt of Bond Street, who, from their acquaintance with ancient armour, their knowledge of the nature and use of ancient weapons, and their established reputation in the ordering of all ancient decorations, were better qualified than any other individuals in the kingdom to do justice to the conceptions of the noble earl, by whom their knowledge and talents were put into requisition. The manner in which the whole of the details, consigned to them by the Earl of Eglinton, and over which he himself may be said to have presided, showed that this very arduous task had not been put into the hands of incompetent persons. The great experience, unremitting attention to the most minute portions of the great whole, laborious patience and minute investigation requisite to make the Tournament a perfect imitation of the Tournaments of earlier days, directed and assisted by the fine taste and accurate judgment of his lordship, produced a result which has never been equalled either in the general grandeur of its conception and execution, in the correctness of its accessories, or in the impression which it made upon the feelings of the immense concourse of spectators by whom it was beheld.

No pageant of any sort in modern times has equalled, in its extraordinary and admirable appearance, the procession of the knights, ladies, barons, men-at-arms, and retainers, from the gates of Eglinton Castle to the appointed lists in the park of that noble domain. It was not a theatrical representation got up for the hour, to captivate and deceive the eye, but it was an actual representation of a real event. The noble personages who were the most conspicuous in the gorgeous throng were the exalted, the brave, and the beautiful of the land; the *élite* of a great empire, not personating in sportive mimicry the character of their illustrious ancestors, but in their own names, and titles, and characters, performing those parts for the time upon the great stage of the world, which those ancestors had performed before them, and in a manner, bringing back to Eglinton Castle the reality as well as the reminiscence of the fifteenth and sixteenth centuries.

The " passages of arms" in the lists were something much beyond mere imitations of the ancient joust,—they were the joust itself, regulated by the laws of ancient chivalry; and, though conducted with that good feeling, and that proper attention to security and to humanity, by which true nobles and true knights are ever distinguished, they were by no means " child's play;" thrusts were given and received with the force and hardihood of the chivalry of the days of the Edwards and the Henrys; and, though to those who did not witness the " courses," it may be deemed an easy matter to contend in friendly rivalry with lance and sword, it is well known to all who were beholders of the contests, that nothing but physical strength, activity, long practice in the use of weapons; and an admirable seat on horseback, united to personal courage and the power of endurance, could enable any candidate for knightly reputation to undergo the trial to which these brave and noble gentlemen were subjected.

In the " mêlée," the strength, and skill, and horsemanship of the combatants were put to a severe trial. If the combat were not an actual struggle for life and death, it was a combat for honour and knightly reputation; and, though restrained by the excellent rules laid down by Lord Eglinton, and admirably carried into effect by Sir Charles Lamb, the Knight Marshal of the Lists, to whom the highest praise is due, it was a contest in which many hard blows were given and received with such hearty good will and such unflinching courage, that no mere field-day warrior, or silken soldier, would have felt himself secure, even within the panoply of plaited mail.

He who engaged in this warlike exercise was certainly—
" No carpet knight so trim,
　But in close fight a champion grim,"

and one who, in his own person, and by his own prowess, bore evidence to the fact, that the descendants of the ancient nobility and gentry of the three great kingdoms of England, Scotland, and Ireland, have by no means degenerated from their brave and hardy ancestry.

The motives of the Earl of Eglinton, and the feelings and recollections of his boyhood and youth, which operated to induce him to plan and carry out this splendid Tournament, cannot be better explained than in the words of his lordship himself, uttered on the occasion of his health being drunk at the banquet, got up in honour of him by the inhabitants of Irvine, on Tuesday, the 29th of September.

After the usual loyal and patriotic toasts had been given, the chairman said the next toast he had to propose, fortunately for him, required no preface—" The health of the Earl of Eglinton." (Great applause.) He knew very well they did not come to hear him speak, and he should therefore not detain them, or offend the ears of the noble guest, by attempting to recapitulate the numerous virtues and excellencies which so conspicuously adorn his character. (Cheers.) His lordship, he might shortly say, in his uniform deportment in private and in public, had gained a seat in the affections of his countrymen such as had seldom fallen to the lot of any other nobleman; and well might this be the case, for truly there was a magnanimity and generosity of soul, a great nobility of mind, which no language could describe, deeply engraven on the whole character and actions of the Earl of Eglinton. (Cheers.) He begged, therefore, to propose—" The health of the Honourable the Earl of Eglinton, and long and happily may he live to be an ornament to the noble house which he represents, a kind landlord, and a blessing and an honour to the country with which he is connected." (Immense cheering.) The toast was drank with all the honours, and reiterated applause.—" There's nae luck about the house."

Lord Eglinton, in rising, was received with renewed plaudits, and, when the cheering had subsided, his lordship spoke as follows :—

Mr. Provost and Gentlemen,—It is with feelings of no ordinary nature, that I rise to return you my thanks for the honour you have just paid me, and for the most gratifying manner in which it has been done. (Cheers.) It is, at all times, most pleasing to receive the approbation of those whose applause we covet; and I will venture to say, that there never was an occasion on which it has been more unsparingly, or more cordially dealt out than at present, or where it has been bestowed on one who felt more sincerely gratified for the kindness of which he is the object. (Cheers.) Whether it is the universal good wishes with which the morning of my life was greeted by many of those whom I see around me, or the kind allowances with which my passage through it has been met; whether it is the manner in which my late attempt to revive amusements which have been so long laid aside, has been met; and last, though not least—whether it is the most gratifying occasion, where I see around me an assembly such as has seldom met to pay honour to any private individual—an assembly of those whom I honour and esteem as my friends, my neighbours and my fellow-countrymen—all contributes to render me most deeply grateful, and to make me unable to thank you in terms such as your kindness merits, or my own heart would dictate. (Loud and repeated cheers.) In this late attempt, I cannot but feel that I do not deserve the praises that have been bestowed upon me; and I must ascribe the honour that has been this evening paid me, not to my own merits, but to the partiality which friendship engenders, and more particularly to the kind feeling which I have invariably met with from the inhabitants of this town. I cannot ascribe it to the Tournament, or to my conduct during it, but to a desire to seize upon the first opportunity which might occur of testifying your friendship towards me. (Cheers.) There is an additional source of gratification which I cannot help adverting to; for, though unhappily it is, in these times, one which but rarely occurs, I most sincerely think it is a circumstance which is an earnest of future unanimity and good will. (Cheers.) I rejoice to see that on this occasion all party feeling—all political rancour has been laid aside; and seeing, as I do, among my kind entertainers of this day, many who are opposed to me in politics, I feel that they must give me that credit which I most freely and gladly accord to them—the credit of conscientiously supporting that cause which I consider most advantageous to my country, without allowing it to interfere with my private friendship. If we differ in our opinions we do not differ in our feelings towards each other—those feelings of kindliness which ought to subsist between man and man, and more especially between those whose views, whose country, whose interests are the same. (Cheers.) I need not, I trust, tell you that it was with no wish of bringing credit on myself, that I commenced the undertaking which has been the cause of this festival—that the marks of approbation which I have received are as unexpected as they are undeserved. (Cheers.) In common with, I believe, a large proportion of my fellow-creatures, I have long looked back to the age of chivalry with admiration, and regretted that the sports which distinguished it, as well as the courtesy and high feeling which were the principal features of the knightly character, now existed only in the page of history, or the legends of romance. (Cheering.) I have pored, when a boy, over the exploits of King Arthur, and the Knights of the Round Table, till I would have given up my bright hopes of future years for the grave that enclosed the glories of a Sir Tristram or a Sir Launcelot. (Great cheering.) In my later years, I have pondered over the pages of Froissart till I fancied I heard the clang of armour and the shrill blast of the trumpet calling me to the tented field—(cheers)—and I have awoke from my dream of chivalry, to find myself in a more refined, but a most unromantic age—(cheers)—where all but dull reality is scoffed at, and imagination must confine herself to the every-day occurrences of modern life. (Cheers.) Can it be wondered at that I endeavoured to realize what was the dream of my boyhood, and the admiration of my riper years—that I wished to see myself, and to show to others, the sports of chivalry as much as the customs of our time would permit? (Cheers.) Can it be wondered at, with these feelings, that, in spite of the difficulties which surrounded it, the danger urged by some, the folly attributed to it by nearly all—(no, no)—I have brought it to a conclusion—a conclusion which, though not such as my most sanguine hopes might have anticipated, still has gained the partial approbation of many of those who witnessed it, and has obtained for me the honour for which I have this day to thank you? (Great cheering.) I am aware of the manifold deficiencies in its exhibition—more perhaps than those who were not so deeply interested in it; I am aware that it was a very humble imitation of those scenes which my imagination had portrayed, but I have, at least, done something towards the revival of chivalry, and I have shown that the sports of a gentle passage of arms can be carried on in the present age, and without any serious danger. (Cheers.) I know (and none have felt it more keenly than myself) that the crash of knights armed with weapons of destruction was wanting—that there was a tameness in the exhibition, when deprived of danger, which lessened its interest; and the care taken to avoid it was perhaps greater than necessary, or than I myself intended, but it was the right side to err on, and I necessarily felt that it was incumbent on me to provide against any serious consequences arising to those whom I had induced to join me in the undertaking. (Cheers.) Assailed as I was on all sides—denounced as a prize-fighter by some—(no, no, and laughter)—threatened with a jail by others, remonstrated with even by those who had the power to put a stop to the exhibition of it altogether, it cannot be wondered at that caution was carried almost to an extreme. I have, I believe, been censured for the waste of money, which might have been better bestowed upon religious or charitable purposes. I humbly conceive that I could not have more profitably employed it than in providing an innocent and interesting amusement which was open to all classes; and by bringing together a concourse of strangers, such as no other means would have collected,—causing an expenditure far exceeding what I could individually have been capable of, and which I trust has proved most beneficial to this town and the neighbourhood. (Great applause.) I cannot but hope that this attempt of mine will be followed, when I see the kindness with which it has been received; and the enthusiasm which has been shown towards it by the inhabitants of this town increases my confidence. (Cheers.) In the reign of King Edward III. a passage of arms was proclaimed, in which the Lord Mayor of London and the Aldermen were to hold the lists against all comers. It was one of the best conducted and most chivalrous Tournaments on record, and the civic dignitaries were triumphant. It is further reported, that when the victorious knights were brought forward to receive the pledge of their valour, it was discovered that the King himself, his two sons, with some of his noblest knights, had occupied the place of the challengers, and had earned glory for the London magistrates. It was, however, by no means uncommon for the chief magistrates of towns to take an interest in, and even participate in these amusements; and Sir William Walworth, a Lord Mayor of London, was one of the most valiant knights on record. May we not, therefore, hope that such examples as these will be followed? May we not hope to witness such scenes as these enacted here? May we not hope to see my worthy friend the Provost don his armour, and hie him to the field, and to hail him as the victor in the lists of chivalry? (Greater laughter, and applause.) If, however, he prefers to follow the example I have cited, and should wish to win the smile of beauty by proxy, I beg to offer myself as a most willing, though unworthy substitute. (Cheers.) If I am wrong in these anticipations—if the spirit of chivalry has slept too long to be again awakened—if armour must no longer clothe the brave and free, but be gaped at only as the trophies of what our ancestors were, and what their descendants must no longer be—still do I rejoice that the attempt has been made,—not only because it has partially succeeded—not only because it has been the means of obtaining for me kindness from all classes, such as I can never feel sufficiently grateful for, but because it has exhibited the character of my fellow-countrymen in a manner which can never be forgotten by those who witnessed it. (Cheering.) I was told beforehand that it would be necessary to have a strong force of constables to guard against the unruly proceedings of the multitude—that I ought to have the yeomanry called out. I was told that my parks would be destroyed—my trees pulled to pieces; but I did not believe these forebodings—so the event has proved that I was right. I trusted to the good sense and good feeling of my fellow-countrymen, and most nobly did they answer to my confidence. (Cheers.) The extreme good order preserved by that immense multitude—their good nature through the worst weather and partial disappointment—their patience through long, though unavoidable delay—was such as I will venture to say was never before equalled, and requires to have been seen to be believed. It excited the astonishment, as well as admiration of all who spoke to me on the subject, and invariably drew forth a remark which I consider the most flattering compliment which could be paid to the men of Ayrshire: " This would not have been done anywhere else." (Much applause.) I felt pleasure before in boasting myself a Scotchman—I felt proud of my countrymen; but that pleasure has been added to, pride has been increased by, their conduct on this occasion. (Cheers.) It shows me that any want of unanimity which may have arisen elsewhere has no existence here; and that, while the richer classes act honestly and friendly by their poorer countrymen, they will always find them what I have found them—a contented, an orderly, and a warm-hearted community. (Cheers.) There are few people in my situation who are so intimately—so exclusively connected with their homes as I am. Every interest I have—everything that I possess is centred here. I have no interest unconnected with the country in which I dwell—I have no hopes of future happiness or future comfort except in the friendship and good opinion of those among whom my lot has been cast. (Immense applause.) It is, then, most gratifying to find that my conduct hitherto has been approved of, and to see the hand of friendship extended towards me by those whose friendship it has been the highest object of my life to gain. (Renewed cheering.) Bound to my country before, by every tie of affection and of interest, I am now bound by the additional one of gratitude; and I trust that my future life will show that I in some degree merit that good opinion which I am proud to think I now possess. (Cheers.) Once more I thank you; and when I tell you that I feel most grateful for it, believe me it is not the careless expression of one who thinks not of it, but the deep and sincere feelings of one who appreciates the kindness of which he has been the object. (Cheers.) Before I sit down, I must request you to fill your glasses to a toast which you will have as much pleasure in drinking as I have in proposing—"The health of the Provost and Magistrates of Irvine, and prosperity to the Burgh." Descended as I am from those who have always been on terms of the utmost intimacy with the inhabitants of the town, I beg to say that I yield to none of those who have gone before me in my friendship towards them, and in my wishes for their welfare and happiness.—His lordship sat down amid loud and long continued applause.

These military exercises were in existence at least as early as the times of the second race of the kings of France, as may be seen in the historians and chroniclers of those days. We are told by Nithart, that, in the interview between Charles the Bald, King of France, and his brother Louis, King of Germany, which took place in the city of Strasburg, the nobles' attendants, who formed the respective suites of these two monarchs, combated on horseback, to give proof of their skill in the use of the lance. The Chronicle of Tours, however, attributes the invention of the Tournament to Geofry, Lord of Preuilly, the father of another Geofry, from whom sprung the noble race of the Counts of Vendome. This Geofry died in the year 1067, so that, if this account be correct, the Tournament was introduced eight hundred years ago; but the fact is, that mention is made, by historians, of combats, similar to those practised at the Tournament, before the date of the lifetime of this worthy, and, therefore, the probability is, that to him the combatants were indebted rather for the code of regulations and laws by which the Tournament was governed, than for the invention of the martial pastime itself. From what the best authorities on this subject have advanced, we must confer the honour of having introduced the Tournament on the Normans, that is, on the Normans who ingrafted themselves upon the aboriginal Gauls, or Frenchmen.

By Matthew Paris, the sports of the Tournament, the jousts, &c., are called, "Conflictus Gallia,"—French combats. There is no question that these combats were introduced into this country by the Normans; nor is any mention made of them until the year 1140, during the reign of King Stephen; nor does it appear that any great Tournament was held in England before the year 1194, during the reign of Richard the First. Sir Walter Scott, with that accuracy of description and fidelity to truth by which his writings are so eminently distinguished, has admirably depicted the great "Passage of Arms," at Ashby de la Zouch, in Leicestershire, which was held during the reign of this monarch; and, though the description there given partakes, almost necessarily, of certain modes and regulations of a later age, described in the pages of Froissart, yet it appears, from a close investigation to the works of antiquaries, that the laws by which the combats of Tournaments were governed, received little alteration in the time that elapsed between the reign of the "Lion-hearted King," and the time of the warlike chronicler.

The Tournament seems to have been introduced into Germany about the year 1136: it is true that Modius has given an account of Tournaments having been celebrated in Germany before that date, but his account is evidently a fiction, and not to be relied upon as historical testimony of the fact.

The Tournaments celebrated at Constantinople during the times of the Crusades are confessedly borrowed from the inhabitants of Western Europe, and are of more recent origin than the Tournament of Tours. John Catacuzene admits that these military games were introduced for the first time into the Eastern Empire, in the year 1326, at the celebration of the nuptials of Anne of Savoy, daughter of Amè IV., Count of Savoy, and the youthful Andronicus Paleologus, the Emperor. However, Nicetas and Cinnamus affirm that the Tournament was known in the Eastern Empire as early as the year 1145.

The combats in the Tournament were instituted to make the knights and nobles acquainted with the use of arms; they were, consequently, not actual combats, but combats between persons professing friendly feelings towards each other: we speak of the Tournament, properly so called, and of which this work describes the splendid revival by the Earl of Eglinton. There were certainly instances in which the combats became more serious, and in which the loss of life and limb was intended, and did take place; these were the combats "à l'outrance." Of course, no revival of such scenes was intended in the noble sports at Eglinton Castle, nor were such things, correctly speaking, part and parcel of the Tournament, or recognised by its strict laws: they were the interpolations of barbarism and brutality—the abuses of the practice, and abuses for which the Tournament itself is not answerable. The weapons properly allowable at the Tournament were such as, without some unfortunate accident, against which it was difficult or impossible to guard, could not cause any serious wounds or injuries to the combatants in the lists: both the lances and the swords made use of were blunted; the "glaives curtois," as the name implies, were weapons for the practice of warlike sports amongst combatants who were only anxious to display their address, and who had no feelings of feud or animosity which rendered the spilling of blood a result or consequence to be desired.

But, notwithstanding all the precautions taken to avoid accidents, it not unfrequently happened that the most fatal accidents arose, either from the excitement of the sports themselves, in which the blood of those engaged was stirred up too strongly for a mere display of skill, and the struggle for the mastery became too violent, or, as it sometimes happened, from fitting opportunities presenting themselves to those who had enmity towards each other, to avenge their supposed wrongs. Thus, Henry Knighton, when describing the Tournament which was held at Chalon, in the year 1274, in which the English King Edward, with the English nobles and knights, tilted against the Count de Chalon and the nobles and knights of Burgundy, says that so many were left upon the lists either slain, or wounded, or disabled, that the Tournament was after spoken of as the "little war of Chalon." The histories, indeed, of those days are filled with the relation of fatal accidents. Robert, Count de Guines, lost his life in a Tournament. Robert of Jerusalem, the Earl of Essex, was killed at a Tournament in the year 1216. Florence, Count of Hainault, and Philip, Count of Boulogne and Clermont, were both killed at a Tournament held at Corbie, in the year 1223. The Count de Hollande was slain in the year 1234, at a Tournament held at Nimiguen. Gilbert, Earl of Pembroke, fell in the lists of the Tournament held in the year 1241, and John, Margrave of Brandenburg, lost his life in a Tournament, in the year 1269. The Count of Clermont was dreadfully wounded in a Tournament in 1279. In the year 1289, Louis, son of the Count Palatine of the Rhine, lost his life in the lists; and in 1294, John, Duke of Brabant, was slain in a Tournament. But these instances, and many more, may be traced to the inexpertness of the combatants, the non-observance of the laws of the Tournament, and the concealed ill-will which the combatants bore to each other. They by no means show that the Tournament, under proper regulations, is necessarily a dangerous, much less a deadly sport. Many lives have been lost in foxhunting, yet who would consent to see that noble and national recreation abolished? There is scarcely a manly sport, in the records of which it would not be easy to find numbers of distressing and even fatal accidents; yet it by no means follows, that on that account the sport is to be abandoned. It may be affirmed, without fear of contradiction, and the affirmation will be corroborated by everybody who witnessed the Tournament at Eglinton, that, had the regulations by which Tournaments are governed been, on the occasions at which accidents of the fatal nature above adverted to, enforced with the perseverance, energy, and suavity by which they were enforced by Sir Charles Lamb, the Marshal of the Lists at Eglinton, no such accidents would have taken place, and the annals of the chivalry of former ages would not have presented so sanguinary a transcript of manners.

The want of the proper enforcement of the rules and laws of the Tournament caused many Papal bulls to be launched from the Vatican against their continuance, but in vain. The anathemas of the Roman Pontifs could not restrain the love of noble pastimes in the breasts of men of noble birth and noble aspirations. Amidst all that was said and done at Rome to abolish the Tournament, Charles VI., in the year 1385, held the famous Passage of Arms at Cambray; and in the year 1520, Francis I. held his great Tournament on the plains between Andres and Guines—a Tournament called, from its splendour, the "Field of the Cloth of Gold," at which the English monarch, Henry VIII., then in the meridian of his power and grandeur, "did battle" in the lists, assisted by all the chivalry of England, against the French monarch and his nobles and knights, in the presence of the rank and beauty of the two countries, and amidst crowds of spectators attracted from every part of Europe to witness the feats of the best and bravest of both England and France. These warlike sports were contrived, planned, and regulated by no less a personage than Cardinal Wolsey, who may almost be said to have presided over the fétes, balls, masques, &c., by which the Tournament was distinguished.

The fatal accident which occasioned the death of King Henry II., at a Tournament at Paris, in the year 1559, from a wound in the eye, inflicted by the lance of the Count de Montgommery, in consequence of the helmet of the monarch not being properly secured, for a time rendered these sports unpopular in France; but in England they were still encouraged; and, during the reign of Elizabeth, were both sanctioned and patronised by the royal presence.

The following record will not be uninteresting to those who take delight in the history of the days of chivalry. It is extracted from the dissertations of the learned Du Conge on the history of Saint Louis, and is so characteristic of the subject, and so appropriate, that no apology is necessary for its insertion here.

"We, John, Duke of Bourbon, Count of Clermont, of Foix and of Lisle, Lord of Beaujeu, Peer and Chamberlain of France, being desirous to relieve our idleness and unbend ourself, and to advance our honour by the measure of our arms, thinking thereby to acquire renown, and the grace of which we are servants, have made a vow, and undertaken, accompanied by sixteen knights and squires of name and rank, to wit: Jacques de Chatillon, Admiral of France (he was killed at the battle of Agincourt, in 1415); Jean de Challon (killed at Agincourt); the Lord of Barbazan (this distinguished chevalier was called 'the knight without reproach,' and was subsequently appointed to head six French knights, in a combat fought between them and six English knights, in presence of the English and French armies; he died in 1432, and lies buried in St. Denys); the Lord of Chartel (killed at the siege of Pontoise, in 1441); the Lord of Gaucort; the Lord de la Heuse; the Lord de Gamaches; the Lord de St. Remi; the Lord de Monsurs; Guillaume Bataille; Drout d'Asniere; the Lord de la Fayette; the Lord de Poulargues; the Lord Carmalet; Louis Louis Cocher; squires—Jean du Pont; Louis Cochet; that we will carry, each of us, on our left legs, a fetter lock, and a chain attached thereto— made of gold for those amongst us who are knights, and of silver for those who are esquires—every Sunday for two successive years, beginning with the Sunday next after the date of this our defiance, until we find an equal number of knights and esquires, of rank and arms without reproach, who will meet us altogether in the lists, and fight to the *l'outrance*, in such armour and harness as each shall please to wear, carrying lance, battle-axe, sword and dagger. The *l'outrance* to be until the one becomes the prisoner of the other. Those on our side who shall become prisoners to be released on giving a fetter lock to him by whom captured similar to those we wear. Those on the other side taken prisoners by us to be released, if knights, by giving each a bracelet of gold; if squires, a bracelet of silver. And let it be known, that we, the Duc de Bourbon, when we shall depart for England, or go before the judge appointed over the combat, that it shall be certified to all our companions, that they shall be furnished with such letters from our Lord the King as shall be necessary for their license and leave in this affair. Done at Paris, the first day of January, in the year of grace 1414."

This document is one of the most curious vestiges of the days of chivalry. The combat, to use the phrase of modern times, never " came off," in consequence of the intervention of the battle of Agincourt, in which many of the intended combatants were slain. The brave Duke of Bourbon was himself taken prisoner at that fatal fight, and brought to England, where he died, after an imprisonment of nineteen years.

The Tournament at Eglinton was a revival of these sports. It was, since the grand display of the " Field of the Cloth of Gold," the most magnificent pageant that Europe has ever witnessed. Not only were the combats of the Tournament revived—not only were the joust, the *mêlée*, the fight at barriers with the two-handed swords, the feats of archery, and all the minor sports by which such festivals were distinguished; but there were the banquet, the endless display of magnificence and wealth, the inexhaustible hospitality of ancient days, again displayed in the baronial halls and apartments of the castle; the ball, the dance, the music, and the minstrelsy; and all this adorned by the beauty, and the rank and fashion of the greatest empire in the world, regulated, directed, and carried into all its details by the munificence and admirable taste of the noble earl who presided over all; and to whom the thanks of all, and the gratitude of all are due, for the affording a spectacle which, to say the least of it, can never be surpassed for munificence and grandeur by any other pageant whatever.

The rules of the joust, and of the "mêlée," were so excellent, and so closely in accordance with the rules of ancient days, that it would be a great omission not to present them here. They were as follows:—

RULES OF THE JOUST.

1. No knight to be permitted to ride without having on the whole of his tilting pieces.

2. No knight to ride more than six courses with the same opponent.

3. It is expressly enjoined by the Earl of Eglinton, and must be distinctly understood by each knight upon engaging to run a course, that he is to strike his opponent on no other part than the shield; and that an *atteint* made elsewhere, or the lance broken across, will be judged foul, and advantage in the former course forfeited.

4. Lances of equal length, substance and quality, as far as can be seen, will be delivered to each knight, and none others will be allowed.

    In default of the lances being splintered in any course, the judge will decide for the *atteint* made nearest to the centre of the shield.

ACTIONS WORTHY OF HONOUR.

1. To break the most lances.

2. To break the lance in more places than one.

3. Not to put the lance in rest until near your opponent.

4. To meet point to point of the lances.

5. To strike on the emblazoument of the shield.

6. To perform all the determined courses.

ACTIONS OF DISHONOUR.

1. To break the lance across the opponent.

2. To strike or hurt the horse.

3. To strike the saddle.

4. To drop the lance or sword.

5. To lose the management of the horse at the encounter.

6. To be unhorsed—the greatest dishonour.

    All lances broken by striking below the girdle, to be disallowed.

ACTION MOST WORTHY.

To break the lance in many pieces.

AT THE TOURNEY OR BARRIER.

Two blows to be given in passing, and ten at the encounter.

These rules were scrupulously adhered to; and to the firmness, tempered with the most knightly suavity of manner, of the Knight Marshal, is to be ascribed the avoidance of anything by which the harmony of the occasion might have been interrupted, from the too great excitement of the moment, or the occurrence of accidents, which a relaxation of his authority might have produced.

In the description with which each plate is accompanied will be read a minute account of the various parts of this great event, that it was deemed unnecessary to place in the introductory portion. It will, however, it is submitted, be proper in this place to give the programme of the procession to the lists as officially set forth by the high functionary who presided.

THE EGLINTON TOURNAMENT

THE OFFICIAL PROGRAMME

OF

THE PROCESSION TO THE LISTS.

MEN AT ARMS,
In Demi-Suits of Armour.

TRUMPETERS,
In full Costume—the Trumpets and Banners emblazoned with the Arms of the Lord of
the Tournament.

TWO DEPUTY MARSHALS,
In Costumes of Blue and White, on foot.

Attendants on foot.

The Eglinton Herald,
In a richly embroidered Tabard.

TWO PURSUIVANTS,
In emblazoned Surcoats.

THE BAND.
Halberdiers of Lord Eglinton.

MEN AT ARMS.
Two Men at Arms of the Knight Marshall of the Lists.

The Herald of the Tournament,
In his Tabard, richly emblazoned with emblematical devices.

MEN AT ARMS,
In Demi-Suits of Armour.

HALBERDIERS,
On foot, in the Livery of the Lord of the Tournament, carrying Halberds.

Officer of the Halberdiers,
On horseback, in a Suit of Demi-Armour, with a gilt Partisan.

RETAINERS,
On foot, carrying heavy steel Battle-axes.

The Judge of Peace,
(Lord Saltoun,)
In his Robes, and bearing a Wand, on a Horse richly caparisoned.

Ladies Visitors.
Lady Montgomerie.

Page.
Sir William Don.

Page.
Mr. F. Ferguson.

LADIES ATTENDING ON LADY MONTGOMERIE.
Miss Margesson, Lady Sarah Saville, Miss Macdonald,
On Horses caparisoned with Blue and White Silk, embroidered with Gold and Silver, each led
by a Groom in Costume of their Colours.

The Knight=Marshal of the Lists,
(Sir Charles Lamb, Bart.,)

Groom.
In a rich embroidered Surcoat, and embossed and gilt Suit of
Armour, his Horse richly caparisoned.

Groom.

Esquire.
Lord Chelsea.

Esquire.
Major M'Dowal.

ATTENDANTS OF THE KNIGHT-MARSHAL,
In Costumes of his Colours, Blue, White, and Gold.

HALBERDIERS OF THE KNIGHT-MARSHAL,
In the Livery of his Colours, with their Halberds.

The King of the Tournament,
(Marquess of Londonderry,)

Halberdier.
In his Robes of Velvet and Ermine, and wearing his Coronet,
his Horse richly caparisoned.

Halberdier.

Esquire.
H. Irvine, Esq.

HALBERDIERS,
In Liveries.

The Irvine Archers,
In Costumes à la Robin Hood,
Captain Grahame, of Glenny.

The Ballochmyle Lady Archers.

Lady Georgiana Douglas.	The Honourable Miss Cathcart.
Miss E. Fergusson, Kilkerran.	Miss Honison Craufurd, Craufurdland.
Miss M'Leod, M'Leod.	Miss Farquhar Gray, Gilmilscroft.
Misses Hamilton, Belleisle.	Misses Hamilton, Sundrum.
Miss J. Cunningham, Caprington.	Miss Helen Houston.

Miss Hunter, Doonholm.

The Queen of Beauty,
(Lady Seymour,)
In a rich Costume, on a Horse richly caparisoned; her Horse led by two Noblemen.

The Marquess of Douglas.   The Marquess of Abercorn.

LADIES ATTENDING ON THE QUEEN,
In rich Costumes.

Countess of Charleville.
Lady Jane Hamilton.

Mrs. Garden Campbell.
Miss Upton.

PAGES OF THE QUEEN,
In Costumes of her Colours.

Esquire.
Hon. F. Charteris.

Esquire.
James Graham, Esq.

The Ayrshire Archers,
In Costumes of Lincoln Green, Black Velvet Baldrick, Rondelle, &c.

Leading the Horses of the Ladies Attendant on the Queen.

Captain.
Claude Alexander, Esq.

Lord Kelburne.	A. Cunningham, Esq.
Sir Robert Dallas.	C. S. Buchanan, Esq.
Captain Blair.	Sir A. Hamilton, Bart.
Stuart Hay, Esq.	Captain Montgomerie.
J. Brownlow, Esq.	J. Burnett, Esq.
— Hamilton, Esq.	Honourable J. Strangways.
Captain Blane.	George Rankin, Esq.

The Jester,
(Mr. M'Ian,)
In a characteristic Costume; bearing his Sceptre; on a Mule, caparisoned and trapped
with Bells, &c.

RETAINERS.

RETAINERS OF THE LORD OF THE TOURNAMENT.

HALBERDIERS OF THE LORD,
In Liveries of his Colours.

Man at Arms,
In Half-Armour.

THE GONFALON,
Borne by a Man at Arms.

Man at Arms,
In Half-Armour.

The Lord of the Tournament,
(The Earl of Eglinton,)

Groom.
In a Suit of gilt Armour, richly chased; on a barbed Charger,
Caparisons, &c., of Blue and Gold.

Groom.

The Banner,
Borne by Lord A. Seymour.

Esquire.
F. Cavendish, Esq.

Esquire.
G. M'Doual, Esq.

RETAINERS OF THE LORD.

6

HALBERDIERS OF THE KNIGHT OF THE GRIFFIN,
In Liveries of his Colours.

MAN AT ARMS, In Half-Armour.	THE GONFALON, Borne by a Man at Arms.	MAN AT ARMS, In Half-Armour.

The Knight of the Griffin,
(THE EARL OF CRAVEN,)

GROOM.	In a Suit of engraved Milanese Armour, inlaid with Gold, on a barbed Charger, caparisoned, &c., in Scarlet, White, and Gold.	GROOM.

Esquire, THE HON. F. CRAVEN.	The Banner, Borne by a Man at Arms, in Half-Armour.	Esquire, THE HON. F. MACDONALD.

RETAINERS.

HALBERDIERS OF THE KNIGHT OF THE DRAGON,
In Liveries of his Colours.

MAN AT ARMS, In Half-Armour.	THE GONFALON, Borne by a Man at Arms.	MAN AT ARMS, In Half-Armour.

Arabian Physician, LORD INGESTRIE.	Confessor, R. MANDEVILLE, Esq.	Pilgrim, C. PRICE, Esq.

The Knight of the Dragon,
(THE MARQUESS OF WATERFORD,)

GROOM.	In a Suit of polished steel fluted German Armour, on a barbed Charger; Caparisons, &c., Black and White.	GROOM.

Page, LORD JOHN BERESFORD.	The Banner, Borne by a Man at Arms.	Page, MARK WHYTE, Esq.

Esquire, SIR CHARLES KENT, BART.		Esquire, J. L. RICARDO, Esq.

RETAINERS.

HALBERDIERS OF THE KNIGHT OF THE BLACK LION.

MAN AT ARMS, In Half-Armour.	THE GONFALON, Borne by a Man at Arms.	MAN AT ARMS, In Half-Armour.

The Knight of the Black Lion,
(VISCOUNT ALFORD,)

GROOM.	In a Suit of polished steel Armour, on a Charger; Caparisons, &c., Blue and White.	GROOM.

Esquire, THE HON. C. H. CUST.	The Banner, Borne by a Man at Arms.	Esquire, T. O. GASCOIGNE, Esq.

RETAINERS.

MAN AT ARMS, In Half-Armour.	THE GONFALON, Borne by a Man at Arms.	MAN AT ARMS, In Half-Armour.

The Knight of Gael,
(BARON GLENLYON,)

GROOM.	In a Suit of polished steel Armour, on a barbed Charger; Caparisons, &c., of Green, Blue, and Crimson. Attended by the ATHOLL HIGHLANDERS, Commanded by The Hon. JAMES PLANTAGENET MURRAY, JOHN MURRAY DRUMMOND, Esq. and CHARLES HOME DRUMMOND, Esq.	GROOM.

Esquire. SIR DAVID DUNDAS, BART.	The Banner, Borne by a Man at Arms.	Esquire. JOHN BALFOUR, Esq.

RETAINERS OF THE KNIGHT OF THE DOLPHIN.

MAN AT ARMS, In Half-Armour.	THE GONFALON, Borne by a Man at Arms.	MAN AT ARMS, In Half-Armour.

The Knight of the Dolphin,
(EARL OF CASSILIS,)

GROOM.	In a Suit of polished steel Armour, inlaid with Gold, on a barbed Charger; Caparisons, &c., Scarlet, Black, and White.	GROOM.

RETAINERS OF THE KNIGHT OF THE RAM.

THE GONFALON,
Borne by a Man at Arms.

The Knight of the Ram,
(THE HON. HENRY HALL GAGE,)

GROOM.	In a Suit of polished steel Armour, on a barbed Charger; Caparisons, &c., Blue, White, and Crimson.	GROOM.

Esquire, R. MURRAY, Esq.	The Banner, Borne by a Man at Arms.	Esquire, R. FERGUSSON, Esq.

MAN AT ARMS, In Half-Armour.	THE GONFALON, Borne by a Man at Arms.	MAN AT ARMS, In Half-Armour.

The Black Knight,
(WALTER LITTLE GILMOUR, ESQ.,)
Without Esquire or Retainers, and with no Device on his Shield; clothed in a Suit of black Armour, and mounted on a black Horse, richly caparisoned.

The Knight of the Swan,
(THE HON. EDWARD STAFFORD JERNINGHAM,)

GROOM.	In a Suit of polished steel Armour, on a barbed Charger; Caparisons, &c., Crimson and White.	GROOM.

Esquire, CAPTAIN STEPHENSON.	The Banner, Borne by a Man at Arms.	Esquire, GARDEN CAMPBELL, Esq.

RETAINERS OF THE KNIGHT OF THE GOLDEN LION,
In Liveries of his Colours.

HALBERDIERS,
In emblazoned Costumes, bearing Halberds.

MAN AT ARMS, In Half-Armour.	THE GONFALON, Borne by a Man at Arms.	MAN AT ARMS, In Half-Armour.

The Knight of the Golden Lion,
(JAMES OGILVIE FAIRLIE, ESQ.,)

GROOM.	In a Suit of richly gilt and emblazoned Armour; Caparisons, &c., Blue and Crimson.	GROOM.

Page.	The Banner, Borne by C. Cox, Esq.	Page.

Esquire, CAPTAIN PURVES.		Esquire, CAPTAIN PETTAT.

HALBERDIERS. RETAINERS.

The Banner,
Borne by R. CRAWFURD, Esq.

The Knight of the White Rose,
(CHARLES LAMB, ESQ.,)
In a Suit of polished steel Armour, on a barbed Charger; Caparisons, &c.,
Blue and Gold Lozenge.
Attended by the ARCHER GUARD, in the costume of their Knight;

Esquire, J. GORDON, Esq.	Captain, PATRICK GORDON, Esq.	Esquire, W. CAMPBELL, Esq.
GROOM.		GROOM.

THE GONFALON,
Borne by a Man at Arms.

The Knight of the Burning Tower,
(SIR F. HOPKINS, BART.,)

GROOM.	In a Suit of polished steel Armour, on a Charger; Caparisons, &c., Black and Gold.	GROOM.

The Banner,
Borne by a Man at Arms.

RETAINERS OF THE KNIGHT OF THE RED ROSE.

THE GONFALON,
Borne by a Man at Arms.

The Knight of the Red Rose,
(R. LECHMERE, ESQ.,)

GROOM.	In a Suit of fluted German Armour, on a barbed Charger; Caparisons, &c., Scarlet and White.	GROOM.

The Banner,
Borne by CORBET SMITH, Esq.

Esquire,
C. CORRY, Esq.

The Knights Visitors,
In ancient Costumes.

PRINCE LOUIS NAPOLEON BONAPARTE.	LORD OSSULSTON.
THE DUKE OF MONTROSE.	LORD SEAHAM.
COUNT ESTERHAZY.	LORD SEYMOUR.
VISCOUNT PERSIGNY.	LORD FITZHARRIS.
LORD MAIDSTONE.	LORD DRUMLANRIG.

SWORDSMEN,
In characteristic Costumes, on foot, each bearing a two-handed Sword on his right shoulder.

BOWMEN,
With Hoods and Bows.

THE SENESCHAL OF THE CASTLE,
In his Costume of Office, bearing his Wand.

TWO DEPUTY MARSHALS,
In Costumes, on horseback.

ATTENDANTS OF THE DEPUTY MARSHALS.

CHAMBERLAINS OF THE HOUSEHOLD,
In Costumes of Office, each bearing his Key.

SERVITORS OF THE CASTLE.

MEN AT ARMS.

THE EGLINTON TOURNAMENT.

PROCESSION TO THE LISTS.

DESCRIPTION OF PLATE—No. I.

"The neighing of the generous horse was heard,
  For battle by the busy groom prepared,
  Rustling of harness, rattling of the shield,
  Clattering of armour, furbish'd for the field,
  Crowds to the Castle, mounted up the street,
  Battering the causeway with their coursers' feet;
  The greedy sight might there devour the gold
  Of glittering arms, too dazzling to behold:
  And polish'd steel that cast the view aside;
  And crested morions, with their plumy pride.
  Knights, with a long retinue of their squires,
  In gaudy liveries march, and quaint attires.

One bore the helm, another held the lance;
  A third the shining buckler did advance.
  The courser paw'd the ground with restless feet,
  And snorting foam'd, and champ'd the golden bit.
  The smiths and armourers on palfreys ride,
  Files in their hands, and hammers at their side,
  And nails for loosen'd spears, and thongs for shields provide.
  The yeomen guard the way, in seemly bands;
  And clowns come crowding on, with cudgels in their hands."

DRYDEN.

BY one o'clock on the appointed day—a day that will long be remembered, not only in Scotland, but throughout most parts of England, Ireland, and Wales, all of which sent their chivalrous levies to the great " Passage of Arms,"

"And noble minds of knights allied were
  In brave pursuit of chivalrous emprise,"—

the trumpets sounded to horse, and the procession to the lists began to form in front of the Castle. It was such a scene as has been seldom witnessed in modern days, but it was one that brought before the eyes of the thousands of spectators assembled in the park, a living transcript of a glorious age. All was bustle, excitement, and animation—

"Arms on armour clashing, bray'd
  Horrible discord."

The procession was formed without confusion, and with a celerity that showed how well the repeated drillings of the knights and esquires, during the spring of the year, in the tilting ground north of the New Road, had trained them for actual service, and how excellently the arrangements, under the orders of the Marshal of the Lists, were carried into execution by the Deputy Marshal, and their subordinate officers.

This Plate represents the procession setting out from the Castle to the Lists, and is as faithful a representation of the commencement of the spectacle as can be well imagined, or as the art of drawing can convey of an actual scene. On the left of the Plate is seen a group of men-at-arms, four abreast; they carry the formidable lances used in the wars of the fourteenth, fifteenth, and sixteenth centuries, by the European soldiery, and still used in warfare by the natives of the north-eastern countries of Europe, and by the native military of many parts of Asia. These men are sheathed in steel, but it will be seen that their armour is not of the same kind as that worn by the knights or esquires; neither are they furnished with swords, such weapons being, on the occasion of tournaments at least, considered superfluous. It will also be seen that they have no surcoats; the surcoat being, properly, the garment of a knight worn over his armour, and emblazoned with armorial bearings, or the device by which the knight is to be known or recognised. The trumpeters, who follow next in the procession, are in the rich costumes of the days of chivalry, but wear neither helmets, back or breast plates. On foot are the Deputy Marshals of the Lists, whose office is to keep order, and attend to the details of the arrangements of the Marshal of the Tournament, and see that all the regulations are obeyed to the letter. On this occasion, the Deputy Marshals did their duty in an admirable manner, and performed a very difficult and complicated task in a way that gave universal satisfaction. On the right on the Plate, this portion of the procession is brought up by the Eglinton Herald and his Pursuivants, habited in the costly costumes, or tabards, by which such functionaries are distinguished, and which are peculiar to their office.

—— "The pursuivants came next,
And, like the heralds, each his scutcheon bore."

In the back ground of this Plate the battlements of Eglinton Castle are seen distinctly. The present edifice is not of great antiquity; it is, indeed, a comparatively modern edifice, not more than forty years being elapsed since it was completed, under the directions of the grandfather of the present Earl of Eglinton. It is built upon the site of the ancient Castle, upon a spot of ground that rises a little above the Park by which it is surrounded. The Park itself is nearly a flat, though beautifully diversified by gentle undulations and slopes, and nobly wooded by large forest trees, and watered by the river Lugden, across a bridge, thrown over which stream, the whole procession passed in its way from the Castle to the Lists. The Castle consists of a circular Keep, around which are drawn four curtains, uniting towers at their angles, and pierced with windows, by which the apartments are lit. The interior is exceedingly commodious, uniting, in a great degree, the notions of feudal grandeur, with the more elegant refinements of modern taste, and the requisition of modern habits and customs. There is a noble collection of warlike weapons, and many relics of antiquity, which prove at once the fine taste of the noble owner, and his patriotic recollections and affection for the honour and the glories of his native country.

The frame of the Plate is formed by Cupids, with lances and swords, emblematical of the influence possessed by the god of love over the rougher energies of the warriors, and the devotion due from knights and esquires to the fair dames and damoisels of the age of chivalry. The wreaths are arabesque, and are emblematical of victory and love.

DESCRIPTION OF PLATE—No. II.

" The *Castle* gates out-poured light-armed troops,
In coats of mail and military pride;
In mail their horses clad, yet fleet and strong,
Prancing their riders bore.
The field all iron cast a gleaming brown,
Nor wanted clouds of foot, nor on each horn
Cuirassiers, all in steel, for standing fight.
Such forces met not, nor so *brave* a camp,

When Agrican, with all his northern powers,
Besieged Albracca, as romances tell,
The city of Gallaphrone, from whence to win
The fairest of her sex, Angelica,
His daughter, sought by many prowest knights,
Both Paynim and the peers of Charlemain,
Such and so *glorious* was their chivalry!"

MILTON.

LOSE to the left of this Plate is a portion of the band on horseback, and next to them are the halberdiers of the Earl of Eglinton: they are on foot, and form the body-guard of the lord of the Castle within the walls. The halberdiers are a sort of guard of state, as well as of active war, kept up in former days by the greater barons of the realm: they were generally picked men, and to them was intrusted the immediate protection of the person of the noble by whom they were retained. As is described in the Plate, their garments were embroidered with the arms of him whom they served. The halberds or weapons with which they armed are tremendous instruments of warfare, and capable of inflicting the most deadly wounds; these weapons are also adapted for repelling an attack in passages, corridors, gateways, and narrow avenues and approaches, and, when used by resolute men trained to their use, will keep at bay a vast body of assailants, and prevent all ingress to the inner apartments of a castle or fortress. It was with weapons of this sort that the halberdiers, who form the body-guard of the Queen of Spain, and who are stationed within the palace, defended the bedroom of her most Catholic Majesty on the occasion of the late attack, and succeeded in repulsing the insurgents from the palace and securing the safety of their mistress. The dresses of the halberdiers represented in this Plate are very appropriate: they are embroidered with the arms of the Earl of Eglinton, which will be described hereafter. The halberdiers are followed by a group of men-at-arms in morions and breast and back-plates of polished steel, having drawn swords in their hands, and wearing buff boots, made of strong leather, of the seventeenth century, instead of the steel greaves of an earlier age. Boots of this sort are of great strength, the buff, or leather, being frequently so tough as to resist a sword cut. It will be observed, that these men have swords, and are not armed with lances. This departure from the usual mode of arming is allowable, and was adopted for the purpose of showing the great diversity of arms made use of at the Tournament. They are followed by two of the retainers of the Knight Marshal of the Lists, in the warlike costume of the sixteenth century, or early part of the seventeenth.

The devices around the Plate represent Cupids, with military weapons and musical instruments, emblematical of the union of Mars with Venus, and of the influence of music both to arouse to war and soothe to peace.

PROCESSION TO THE LISTS. N°2

DESCRIPTION OF PLATE—No. III.

Sir Charles Montolieu Lamb, Baronet, Knight Marshal of the Lists.

" Not long I had observed, when from afar
   I heard a sudden symphony of war;
   The neighing coursers, and the soldiers' cry,
   And sounding trumps that seem'd to tear the sky:
   I saw, soon after this, behind the grove
   From whence the ladies did in order move,
   Come issuing out in arms a warrior train,
   That like a deluge pour'd upon the plain;
   On barbed steeds they rode, in proud array."

" To tell their costly furniture were long,
   The summer's day would end before the song.

" The trumpets issued, in bright mantles dress'd,
   A numerous troop.

" And at each trumpet was a banner bound,
   Which, waving in the wind, display'd at large
   Their masters' coat of arms, and, knightly charge,
   The chief about their necks the scutcheons wore.

" Next these of kings-at-arms a goodly train
   In proud array came prancing o'er the plain;
   Their cloaks were cloth of silver mix'd with gold.
   The pursuivants came next, in number more,
   And, like the heralds, each his scutcheon bore.

" The henchmen were for every knight assign'd,
   All in rich liveries clad, and of a kind.
   The foremost held a helm of rare device—
   A prince's ransom would not pay the price.
   The second bore the buckler of his knight;
   The third of cornel wood a spear upright,
   Headed with piercing steel, and polish'd bright.
   Like to their lords their equipage was seen.

" At length there issued from the grove behind,
   A fair assembly of the female kind."

CHAUCER, BY DRYDEN.

DRESSED in the costume of the halberdiers of the Knight Marshal of the Tournament is seen a group of hardy retainers of that important functionary. They are to the left hand of the Plate, and close to them comes the herald of the Knight Marshal in his splendid tabard, attended by a trumpeter. A standard-bearer, with the banner of Sir Charles Montolieu Lamb, follows; on the banner the arms of the baronet are emblazoned. Lord Chelsea and Major Mac Doual, the Esquires of the Knight Marshal, accompanied by Sir Hugh Campbell, follow next. Ladies attending the Tournament are then seen on horseback, clothed in the elegant costumes of the age of Elizabeth and Mary Queen of Scots: the dresses are of velvet, trimmed with ermine, and the caps the tasteful head-gear of the end of the sixteenth century. The ladies represented by the painter are Miss Mac Donald, Lady Sarah Saville, and Miss Margesson. After them comes Lord Saltoun, the Judge of Peace, an important officer at all Tournaments, and whose duty it was to maintain peace and decide between disputants. His lordship is habited in the robes of his office, with cap and plume. This nobleman, Alexander George Fraser, is Baron Saltoun of Abernethy, and sits in the House of Lords as a representative peer of Scotland. He succeeded to his title as sixteenth baron on the death of his father, in **1793.** He is a colonel in the army, Companion of the Bath, a Military Knight of Russia and Austria, and was an aide-de-camp to his late Majesty William the Fourth. The pages on foot of Lady Montgomerie follow, Sir William Henry Don of Newtondon, in the county of Berwick, Bart., and Frederick William Brown Fergusson, Esq., eighth son of Sir James Fergusson of Kilkerran, in Ayrshire, Bart., by his second wife, Henrietta, second daughter of the celebrated conqueror at Camperdown, Admiral Lord Duncan. The lady seen between the pages is the Lady Montgomerie.

Sir Charles Montolieu Lamb, the Knight Marshal of the Tournament, with a posse of halberdiers, is seen on the right hand of the Plate. The suit of armour worn by the honourable baronet was one of the most splendid and elaborate displayed on the occasion. The representation in the Plate is correct even to the minuter details. It is what the armourers call a " demi-suit." The workmanship is Venetian. The horse, which the Knight Marshal manages with the skill and grace of an experienced horseman, is represented as armed with the chanfron and manefure, precisely as he appeared in the Lists.

Nothing could have been more judicious than the appointment of Sir Charles Montolieu Lamb to the office of Knight Marshal of the Tournament, and nothing could have been more admirable than the manner in which he discharged the very onerous duties which devolved upon him. His perfect command of temper, his dignified, yet affable demeanour, his firmness in the enforcement of his commands, tempered by the most knightly suavity of manners, were the delight and admiration of all who took part in the passages of this great Tournament; and whilst they operated to the preservation of order, and perhaps of life and limb, secured him the veneration, respect, and applause of every combatant, and of every one of the many thousand spectators who were witnesses of his polite, yet manly, conduct.

The ancient lineage of the noble baronet, and his family connection with the Earl of Eglinton, also pointed him out as the most fitting person for the office he filled. Sir Charles Montolieu Lamb is the great-great-grandson of the celebrated cavalier and royalist, Lieutenant-colonel Robert Burgess, who so nobly defended the town of Farringdon, of which he was the deputy-governor under Colonel Owen, against Oliver Cromwell, and the son of James Bland Burgess, who, after serving as Under-secretary of State for six years, was created a baronet in **1795,** and appointed Knight

Marshal of the King's Household, with a reversion of this office limited to his eldest son. Sir James Bland Burgess, in 1780, married Anne, third daughter of Lieutenant-colonel Montolieu, Baron of St. Hypolite, by whom he had the present baronet, and several other children. Sir James assumed, by royal permission, in 1821, the surname of Lamb, and quartered the arms of Lamb with those of Burgess. He died in 1824, and was succeeded by the present baronet, who married Lady Montgomerie, relict of Archibald Lord Montgomerie, and the mother of the present Earl of Eglinton. At the period of the death of George the Fourth, and the Coronation of William the Fourth, Sir Charles being on the Continent, the office of Knight Marshal on both those occasions was performed by deputy, by George Head, Esq., on whom His Majesty William the Fourth was pleased to confer the honour of knighthood, October 14, 1831, as Deputy Knight Marshal. Sir Charles attended in person, and most efficiently discharged the duties of his office, at the Coronation of Her present Most Gracious Majesty.

In the upper portion of the frame by which the Plate is enclosed, are represented Cupids, with wreaths of flowers and fruits, and the arms of Sir Charles Montolieu Lamb, surmounted with his crest, are appropriately introduced.

ARMORIAL BEARINGS.

SIR CHARLES MONTOLIEU LAMB, Baronet:
Per pale wavy argent and ermines, a chevron between three lambs passant sa. quartering Burgess.
The CREST.—A lamb on a wreath, passant, sa. charged on the body with a bezant, thereon a trefoil slipped vert.
MOTTO.—"Deo et principe."

No. 1.—LORD SALTOUN:
Quarterly: first and fourth azure, three frasers or cinquefoils argent, for Fraser. Second or, a lion rampant gules, debruised, with a riband salient, for Abernethy. Third argent, three piles gules, for Wishart.
CREST.—An ostrich holding in his beak a horse-shoe, all proper.
MOTTO.—"In God is all."
SUPPORTERS.—Two angels with wings expanded and endorsed proper, verted, in long garments or.

No. 2.—LORD CHELSEA:
Quarterly: first and fourth gules, a lion rampant reguardant argent. Second and third argent, three boars' heads couped, salient.
CREST.—Out of a ducal coronet or, a dragon's head vert.
MOTTO.—"Nui invidet minor est."
SUPPORTERS.—Dexter, a lion reguardant or. Sinister, a dragon reguardant vert, each gorged, with a double tressure flory, counterflory, gules.

No. 3.—SIR HUGH CAMPBELL:
A gyrony of eight.
CREST.—A phœnix's head.
MOTTO.—"Constanter et prudenter."

No. 4.—LADY MONTGOMERIE:
The arms here given are those of Sir Charles Lamb; but these are borne conjointly with those of Montgomerie, for which see Plate VI.

No. 5.—MISS MACDONALD:
Quarterly: first and fourth grand quarters quarterly; first argent, a lion rampant gules; second or, a hand in armour holding a cross crosslet fitcheè, gules; third vert, a salmon naiant in fesse proper; fourth argent, a row galley or lymphad, sails furled, sa., for Macdonald. Second and third grand quarters, arms of Bosville.
SUPPORTERS.—Two leopards proper, plain, collared or.
MOTTO.—"Per mare, per terras."

No. 6.—LADY SAVILLE:
Argent, on a bend salient three owls of the field.
SUPPORTERS.—Two lions proper, collared and chained, or.
MOTTO.—"Be fast."

No. 7.—MISS MARGESSON:
Sa. a lion pass. guard. az., a chief engra. or.
MOTTO.—"Loyalté me lie."

No. 8.—MAJOR MAC DOUAL:
First and fourth, a lion rampant; second and third, or, a lymphad sa, with a beacon on the topmast, ppr.
MOTTO.—"Vincam vel moriar."

No. 9.—SIR WILLIAM HENRY DON:
Vert, on a fesse az. three massels sa.
CREST.—A pomegranate proper.
MOTTO.—"Non deerit alter aureus."

No. 10.—FREDERICK WILLIAM BROWN FERGUSSON, ESQ.:
Azure, a buckle az. between three boars' heads couped.
CREST.—A bee upon a thistle.
MOTTO.—"Dulcius ex asperis."

KNIGHT-MARSHAL

OF THE LISTS

SIR CHARLES LAMB, BARONET

PROCESSION TO THE LISTS N°.3.

1. Lord Gillmour. 2. Lord Craven. 3. Sir Hugh Campbell. 4. John Hargreaves. 5. John Hargreaves. 6. Colin Shadwell. 7. Colin Fitzgerald. 8. Walter Aird Powell. 9. The Hon. Hunt. 10. Capt. Gage.

DESCRIPTION OF PLATE—No. IV.

Charles William Vane Stewart, Marquess of Londonderry, King of the Tournament.

" Mounted upon a hot and fiery steed,
   Which his aspiring rider seem'd to know,
   With slow but stately pace kept on his course.

" Noble, courageous, high, unmatchable.

"A rarer spirit never
   Did steer humanity—
   Friend and companion in the front of war."

SHAKSPEARE.

EXTENDING across the whole of the Plate, the procession continues to advance to the Lists. First comes the Marquess of Londonderry, who is represented in his gorgeous robes as King of the Tournament, the highest officer in these chivalric exercises, and one to whom all others were bound to be obedient. This office, in ancient days, was always conferred on one of the highest of the nobility of the realm, or on some great baron who had distinguished himself in the wars and battles of his country, and to whom knighthood was indebted for the support and advancement of its claims, its privileges, and its honours. It would have been impossible to have selected a more appropriate and efficient King of the Tournament to preside over the warlike sports at Eglinton, than the gallant nobleman represented in the Plate. His lordship's military career has been one of glorious enterprise and brilliant success; the companion in arms of the great captain, the Duke of Wellington, and the participator in those hard-fought fields and splendid victories by which the British soldier is exalted beyond all competition in the annals of fame; a nobleman distinguished for his diplomatic services, when his sword, having helped to conquer peace for his country and for the world, was sheathed in the scabbard, to which it had been long a stranger; a nobleman, moreover, distinguished by his unflinching advocacy of everything conducive to the honour and prosperity of his country, and not more eminent as a warrior than a statesman:

"Brave peer of England, pillar of the state,"

and who, to the valour of a soldier, the integrity of a patriot, and the sagacity of a diplomatist, unites the manners and deportment of an accomplished cavalier. The noble Earl supported the dignity of his office most admirably. His appearance, at once commanding, graceful, and knightly, as he managed with the address of an experienced horseman his prancing steed, was hailed with "loud acclaim," and, as he passed through thousands of spectators to his appointed station in the Lists, awoke to admiration and excited to applause the eyes and voices of all beholders. This nobleman, Charles William Vane Stewart, in addition to the title of Marquess of Londonderry, bears the titles of Earl of Londonderry, Viscount Castlereagh, and Baron Stewart, in the Peerage of Ireland; Earl Vane, Viscount Seaham of Seaham, in the county of Durham, and Baron Stewart of Stewart's Court, in the Peerage of the United Kingdom. He was born on the 18th of May, 1778; elevated to the Peerage as Baron Stewart on the 1st of July, 1814; succeeded to his Marquisate, on the death of his lamented brother, on the 12th of August, 1822, and on the 28th of March, 1823, was created Viscount Seaham and Earl Vane, with remainder to his issue male by his second marriage.

The Marquess was married to his first wife, Catherine, youngest daughter of John third, and late Earl of Darnley, on the 8th of August, 1804. That lady died in the year 1812, leaving issue by the Marquess, Frederick William Robert Viscount Castlereagh, M.P., born July 7, 1805. The second and present wife of the Marquess is Frances Anne, only daughter of Sir Harry Vane Tempest, by Anne Catherine, late Countess of Antrim, in her own right.

The noble Earl is escorted by halberdiers on foot, after which group comes H. Irvine, Esq., on horseback with a strong band of the Irvine Archers. This part of the procession was extremely characteristic and in keeping with the sports of the day. A man-at-arms, on foot, salutes as the procession passes, he is armed with a two-handed sword, a fine specimen of its class.

The upper border of this Plate is formed of Cupids, who hold wreaths of flowers, mingled with bunches of fruits; in the centre is the armorial coat of the Marquess of Londonderry, surmounted with a coronet. On the lower frame are represented Cupids with targets, and bows and arrows, emblematic of the office of H. Irvine, Esq., who commands the Irvine Archers. The arms of this gentleman are in the centre.

ARMORIAL BEARINGS.

No. 1.—MARQUESS OF LONDONDERRY:

Quarterly; first and fourth az., three sinister gauntlets or, in chief a trefoil slipped of the last, for Vane; second and third or, a bend compony, ar. and az., between two lions rampant gules, for Stewart.

CRESTS—of Vane, a dexter gauntlet erect, holding a sword proper, pommel and hilt or. :—of Stewart, a dragon statant or.

SUPPORTERS of the Family.—Dexter, a Moor, wreathed about the temples, ar. and az., holding in his exterior hand a shield of the last, garnished or, charged with the sun in splendour or. Sinister, a lion.

SUPPORTERS borne by the present Marquess.—Two hussars of the tenth regiment, the dexter mounted on a grey horse, and the sinister upon a bay horse, with their swords drawn, and accoutred, all proper.

MOTTO.—" Metuenda corolla Draconis."

No. 2.—HENRY IRVINE, ESQ.:

Ar. three holly leaves slippled, vert.

KING OF THE TOURNAMENT.

CHARLES WILLIAM VANE STEWART, MARQUESS OF LONDONDERRY

PROCESSION TO THE LISTS—CONTINUED.

DESCRIPTION OF PLATE—No. V.

Jane Georgiana, Lady Seymour—Queen of Beauty.

" The Nymphes with quivers shall adorne
    Their active sides, and rouse the morne
With the shrill musicke of their horne."
                    JOHN HABINGTON CASTARA.

" Virginibus Tyriis mos est gestare pharetrum,
    Purpureoque alte suras vincire cothurno."
                    ÆNEID, lib. i., 140.

" Qualis in Eurotæ ripis, aut per juga Cynthi
    Exercet Diana choros."
                    IB., 502.

" Then they cast on their gownes of greene,
        And took their bowes each one ;
    And they away to the greene forrest
        A shooting forth are gone."
                    ANCIENT BALLAD.

" ———— In the midst was seen
    A lady of a more majestic mien ;

By stature and by beauty mark'd their sovereign queen.
    Her servants' eyes were fix'd upon her face,
    And, as she moved or turn'd, her motions view'd,
    Her measures kept, and step by step pursued."

" And as in beauty she surpass'd the quire,
    So, nobler than the rest, was her attire.
    A crown of ruddy gold inclosed her brow,
    Plain without pomp, and rich without a show."
                    DRYDEN.

" A fool, a fool ! I met a fool i' the forest,
    A motley fool—a miserable fool !
    As I do live by food, I met a fool ;
    Who laid him down, and bask'd him in the sun,
    And rail'd on lady fortune in good terms,
    In good set terms, and yet a motley fool.
            O noble fool !
    A worthy fool ! motley's the only wear."
                    SHAKSPEARE.

IRST on the left are seen the Ballochmyle Lady Archers, the ladies attendant on the Queen of Beauty, habited in a costume not unusual in the pageants and masques of the middle ages, and adopted even as late as the reigns of Charles and James the Second, and, on this occasion, exceedingly appropriate and picturesque. The names of these ladies will be seen on reference to the official programme, and amidst this group were some of the most lovely of female forms and faces. It was, indeed, a befitting group to wait upon the Queen of Beauty, Lady Seymour. A group of beauties escorting their mistress and monarch to the throne erected for her in the Lists from which she was to issue her commands, distribute the rewards of valour, and with her

" ———— bright eyes
Rain influence and judge the prize"

to the adventurous knights, inspired and animated by the loveliness of the spectacle of the most beautiful of women presiding over a group, where all were beautiful. Lady Seymour, who is seen mounted on the spirited palfrey, which seems enamoured with his burthen, "bore her state well." No lady throughout the empire could have been chosen whose pre-eminent attractions of face and figure, whose elegance of manners, whose correctness of taste and feminine dignity of demeanour, could better have entitled her to the proud rank of "Queen of Beauty." She was, on this occasion, most truly

" the admired of all admirers,"

a glittering star amidst a constellation of the most lovely of the female sex of the most exalted in rank and fashion throughout the British Isles. Her ladyship is the youngest daughter of the late Thomas Sheridan, Esq., eldest son of the Rt. Hon. Richard Brinsley Sheridan, M. P.; was married on the 10th of June, 1830, to Edward Adolphus Lord Seymour, a Lord of the Treasury, M. P., eldest son of Edward Adolphus, St. Maur, Duke of Somerset, and Baron Seymour, in the peerage of England. The palfrey of her ladyship, covered with the richest housings, is led by two of the nobles of the land—the Marquess of Douglas and the Marquess of Abercorn, habited in the Highland costume.

It was very properly arranged that to these two noblemen should be intrusted the honour of conducting the Queen of Beauty to the Lists. The ancient lineages of the families of Hamilton and Douglas, which they respectively represent, exalted the office to which they were appointed, and whilst it did honour to the pageant, evinced that, in the discharge of knightly duties, the highest rank and the most illustrious nobility must yield obedience to the commands of Beauty, and fulfil the *devoirs* which gallantry owes to the fair sex.

The nobleman represented in the Plate—James Hamilton, Marquess of Abercorn—is now in the very prime of life, having been born on the 12th of January, 1811, and enjoys besides the Marquisate of Abercorn, to which he succeeded on the death of his grandfather, in 1818, the titles of Viscount Hamilton, of Hamilton, in the county of Leicester, in the Peerage of England. He is Earl of Abercorn, Baron of Paisley, Abercorn, Hamilton, Mountcastle, and Kilpatrick, in the Peerage of Scotland. Viscount and Baron Strabane ; Baron Mountcastle, in the Peerage of Ireland, and a Baronet of Ireland, and with the exception of the Earl of Verulam, is the only nobleman who has a Peerage in each of the three kingdoms. He is descended from Bernard, kinsman of Rollo, first Duke of Normandy, from whom has descended, through a long series of noble ancestors, the many honours and titles which are borne by his lordship. The Marquess of Douglas and Clydesdale is the son of the Duke of Hamilton. The Hamiltons are descended from Sir Gilbert Hamilton, who flourished in the reign of Edward the Second. Sir Gilbert having slain John De Spencer, in a rencontre, fled from the court of England and sought safety in Scotland.

DESCRIPTION OF PLATE—No. V.—CONTINUED.

The four ladies on horseback who form the next group, are Lady Charleville, Mrs. Garden Campbell, Miss Upton, and Lady Jane Hamilton. The costumes of these ladies were remarkable for the great taste displayed in them, and for the accuracy of style and close attention to the costumes of persons of rank of the age of which they were imitations. This portion of the cavalcade was striking in its effect, and won, from thousands of voices, loud cheers, and hearty approbation. The Ayrshire Archers, commanded by Claude Alexander, Esq., bring up the rear, and on the extreme right is seen the Jester, Mr. M'Ian, whose humour, eccentricity, and ready repartee, filled up, in the most pleasant manner, the intervals between the courses of the Lists, and kept alive the spirit of mirth and revelry throughout the Park and the Castle from morn till "dewy eve," and from eve till morn again. The dress worn by the Jester was well chosen. The character was about midway between the Wamba of Sir Walter Scott and the Touchstone of Shakespeare, a somewhat rustic, somewhat courtly wit, well versed in the Doric of the glades of the North, and yet abounding in the more sharp refinements of the town and city.

Cupids, with cornucopias and bows and arrows, form the upper border of the Plate, and in the midst are emblazoned the arms of the Queen of Beauty. The lower border contains eight other coats of armorial bearings as stated below.

ARMORIAL BEARINGS.

LADY SEYMOUR:

Quarterly: first and fourth or, on a pile gu. between six fleur de lis arg., three lions of England; being the coat of augmentation granted by Henry the Eighth on his marriage with Lady Jane Seymour. Second and third gu. two wings, conjoined in lure, the first downwards, or, for Seymour.

CREST.—Out of a ducal coronet or, a phœnix of the last, issuing from flames, ppr.

SUPPORTERS.—Dexter, a unicorn az. armed, maned, and tufted or, gorged with a ducal collar per pale az. and or, to which is affixed a chain of the last; similar a bull az. ducally gorged, chained, hoofed, and armed or.

MOTTO.—"Foy pour devorie."

No. 1.—MARQUESS OF DOUGLAS:

Quarterly: four grand quarters; first and fourth quarterly, first and fourth gu., three cinque-foils pierced ermine for Hamilton; second and third ar., a ship, with her sails furled, sa., for Arran. A human heart gu., imperially crowned proper, on a chief az., three mullets of the field, for Douglas.

CREST.—A salamander in flames.

MOTTO.—"Jamais arriere."

No. 2.—MARQUESS OF ABERCORN:

Quarterly: first and fourth gules, three cinque-foils, pierced, ermine, for Hamilton; second and third argent, a ship, with sails furled, sable, for the Earls of Arran.

CREST.—Out of a ducal coronet or, an oak, fructed and penetrated transversely in the main stem by a frame saw ppr.; the frame gold.

SUPPORTERS.—Two antelopes ar. horned, ducally gorged, chained and hoofed or.

MOTTOS.—"Through," and "Sola nobilitat virtus."

No. 3.—LADY CHARLEVILLE:

Quarterly: first and fourth vert, a cross crosslet ar., for Bury. Second and third azure, on a chief indented ar., three mullets, gules, a crescent for difference, for Moore.

CREST.—A boar's head, couped transpierced through the mouth with an arrow, ppr.

SUPPORTERS.—Two blacks attired az., wreathed about the temples, ar., and of the first, each holding in his exterior hand a dartl, ppr.

MOTTO.—"Victus sub cruce crescit."

No. 4.—MRS. GARDEN CAMPBELL:

See those of Garden Campbell, Esq., in Plate XI.

No. 5.—LADY JANE HAMILTON:

Gules, three cinque-foils ermine.

MOTTO.—"Viridis et fructifera."

No. 6.—MISS UPTON:

Sa. a cross moline ar.

MOTTO.—"Semper paratus."

No. 7.—HON. F. CHARTERIS:

Quarterly: first and fourth ar., a fesse az., within a double tressure flory counterflory gu. Second and third or, a lion ramp. sa.

CREST.—A swan ppr.

SUPPORTERS.—Two swans ppr.

MOTTO.—"Je pense."

No. 8.—F. GRAHAM, ESQ.:

Or, on a fesse ermine, three eschallops of the first.

CREST.—An eagle.

MOTTO.—"Souvenez."

QUEEN OF BEAUTY. LADY SEYMOUR.
LANE GEORGIANA LADY SEYMOUR.

1 Marquess of Douglas. 2 Marquess of Abercorn. 3 Lady Clinderville. 4 Queen the Imperial. 5 Lady Jane Hamilton. 6 Miss Upton. 7 Hon. E. Graham Esq.
8 Mr. Ballintaulor. Jobst Jenkins. 9 Queen the Imperial.
EGLESDON SUCHEX. IRSS. N° J.

DESCRIPTION OF PLATE—No. VI.

Archibald William Montgomerie, Earl of Eglinton, Lord of the Tournament.

"And by his banner borne is his penon
Of gold ful riche."

CHAUCER'S KNYGHTE'S TALE.

"Sparse al vento on deggiando ir le
bandiere,
Eventolar sa i gran cimier le
penne.
Habiti, fregi, imprese, arme, e
colori."

TASSO. CANT. 20, ST. 28.

"——————— by his light,
Did all the chivalry of England move
To do brave acts; he was indeed the glass

Wherein the noble youth did dress themselves.
——————— So that in speech, in gait,
In diet, in affections of delight,
In military rules, humours of blood,
He was the mark and glass, copy and book,
That fashion'd others.
Second to none,
To look upon the hideous God of War."

SHAKSPEARE.

"——————— His goodly eyes
Over the files and musters of the war
Have glow'd like plated Mars."

SHAKSPEARE.

ATHERED in clusters on the left hand, as the spectator surveys the scene, are halberdiers and bill-men, armed with partisans. Men-at-arms on foot, armed with two-handed swords, weapons of an early date in the history of chivalry, and used in the wars of the crusades with terrible effect against the Paynim warriors in Palestine, come next: then follows the Gonfalon of the Lord of the Tournament borne by a man-at-arms in armour and on horseback. In the centre of the Plate rides, on a noble war-horse, the Earl himself. He wears a splendid suit of armour, of the finest steel plates, engraved and gilt. The effect of this gorgeous suit was very striking; no knight in the whole procession approached in splendour and dignity the appearance of this nobleman. The horse is caparisoned with emblazoned trappings, and armed en suite. Men-at-arms, retainers, &c., close the immediate retinue of their master. Lord A. Seymour, bears aloft the banner of the noble Earl emblazoned with the Eglinton arms. The two esquires, F. Cavendish, Esq., and G. Mac Doual, Esq., follow next, the former carrying the helmet, which is of exquisite workmanship, steel-gilt and burnished, surmounted with the coronet of his lordship, on which are the crest and plume. The Castle of Eglinton is seen in the distance.

This great Earl is descended from ancestry whose names are eminently recorded in the annals of his own country, and the history of great achievements in many parts of the world. He can boast a genealogy, in tracing which the names and deeds of warriors, statesmen, and patriots, are continually presenting themselves, yet, throughout this long list of worthies, no name is to be met with by which the reputation of him who now bears the accumulated honours of his noble house is eclipsed. Archibald Earl of Eglinton, the "Lord of the Tournament," is thus descended.

Roger Montgomery, Vicompte de Hiesmes, commanded the van of the army of the Conqueror at Hastings, in 1066, and for his services was created Earl of Arundel and Shrewsbury, and made tenant in capite of many broad manors in the county of Shropshire, and other parts of England. He subsequently obtained extensive domains in Wales, which, after his Norman name, were called Montgomeryshire. A descendant of this gallant Earl, removed into Scotland about the middle of the twelfth century, and obtained, by grant of the Crown, the manor of Eaglesham in Renfrewshire, which still continues in the family. In the fourteenth century Sir John Montgomery married Elizabeth, daughter of Sir Hugh de Eglinton, heiress to the estates of Englinton and Ardrossan, in Ayrshire, by which marriage those extensive possessions passed into the family of the husband. This Sir John Montgomery fought at the battle of Otterburn, and, as related by Froissart, took prisoner the famous Henry Percy, called Hotspur. The son of Sir John Montgomery, Sir Hugh, is said, according to the account in the ancient ballad of "Chevy Chase," to have been slain in this battle.

"Off all that se a Skottishe knyght,
Was callyd Sir Hewe the Mongon-byrry;
He sawe the Duglas to the deth was dyght;
He spendyd a spear, a trustie tie.

"He rod uppon a corsaire
Throughe a hondrith archery;
He never styntyde, nar never blane,
Tyll he cam to the good Lord Persè.

"He set uppone the Lord Persè
A dynte that was full soare;

With a suar spear of a myghte tre
Clean thorow the body he the Persè bore.

"Athe tothar syde, that a man myght se,
A large cloth yard and mare;
Towe bettar captayns wear nat in Christianye,
Then that day slain wear ther.

"An archer off Northomberlonde
Say slean was the Lord Persè;
He bar a bende-bow in his hande,
Was made of trusti tre.

> "An arow, that a cloth yarde was lang,
> To th' hard stele haylde he ;
> A dynt, that was both sad and sore,
> He sat on Sir Hewe the Mongon-byrry.

> "The dynt yt was both sad and sore,
> That he of Mongon-byrry sete ;
> The swane-fethars that his arrowe bar,
> With his hart blood the wear wete."

The account given in the ancient ballad of the "Battle of Otterbourne," is, however, at variance with this narrative; the minstrel there says,

> "This fraye bygan at Otterborne,
> Bytwene the nyghte and the day ;
> There the Dowglas lost hys lyfe,
> And the Percy was lede awaye.

> "Then was ther a Scottyshe prisoner tayne,
> Sir Hughe Mongomery was hys name;
> For soth as I yow saye,
> He borrowed the Percy home agayne."

Both Sir Hugh and Percy are here described to have been made prisoners, and exchanged the one against the other, which circumstance shows the high estimation in which the former was held, Percy being, as everybody knows, one of the first of the English nobility, and the flower of the English chivalry of that age.

In the year 1448, the family of the Montgomery was raised to the Peerage, with the title of Baron Montgomery, and in the commencement of the sixteenth century, the title of Earl of Eglinton was conferred upon the head of it by James the Fourth of Scotland.

The sixth Earl of Eglinton, Alexander, called "Grey Steel," was one of the most celebrated nobles of his day, he succeeded to the family titles and estates in 1612. He was a formidable opponent to Cromwell in the civil wars, in which he and his four sons were actively engaged. The protector, in revenge, destroyed the ancient Castle of Ardrossan.

The ninth Earl, Alexander, took a leading part in the wars of the Rebellion in 1715, and in conjunction with the Earls of Glasgow, and Kilmarnock, and the Lord Sempill, raised six thousand men at Irvine to assist the government against the Pretender.

The tenth Earl, Alexander, was one of the most celebrated agriculturists of his times, and it is to him that Ayrshire and the western districts of Scotland owe much of the benefits arising from a scientific cultivation of the land. This nobleman came to an untimely death from a wound inflicted by a person who was trespassing on his grounds in the year 1769.

His brother Archibald, the next Earl, raised a regiment of Highlanders in 1757, and accompanied them to North America, where he served with reputation, more especially in an expedition at the head of 1,200 men against the Cherokees. At his death, in 1796, he held the rank of a general in the army.

As his lordship left no sons, the titles, and the greater part of the estates, devolved on Hugh Montgomery of Coilsfield, the male representative of the family, who became twelfth Earl of Eglinton. He entered the army in 1756, served in North America during the greater part of the seven years' war, and was fourteen years a Captain in the First Regiment of Foot, or Royal Scots. In 1778, he was appointed Lieutenant-Colonel of the Argyle Fencibles. In 1793, he raised the West Lowland Regiment, of which he was Colonel, and soon after he raised a regiment of the line, called the Glasgow Regiment, which was reduced in 1795. In 1806, he was created a British Peer, by the title of Baron Ardrossan. His lordship died in 1819.

His son Archibald, Lord Montgomery, was born in 1773. In early life he entered into the army as an Ensign in the 42nd Regiment, or Royal Highlanders. He was Lieutenant-Colonel of the Glasgow Regiment, reduced in 1795; and afterwards Colonel of the Ayrshire Militia, which he resigned in 1807. He was promoted to the rank of Major-General in the army in 1809. He served in Sicily in the years 1812 and 1813, where, in the absence of Lord William Bentinck, he represented his Britannic Majesty at the Court of Palermo. Removing thence, on account of bad health, he died, in 1814, at Alicant in Spain. His lordship married Lady Mary Montgomery, eldest daughter of Archibald, eleventh Earl of Eglinton, thus uniting the lineal and the male branches of the family. The present Earl is the only surviving child of this marriage. He was born in 1812; received the name of Archibald William; and in 1819 succeeded his grandfather in the titles and the estates.

Since the celebration of the "Tournament" his lordship married, Feb. 17, 1841, Mrs. Theresa Newcomen, widow of Richard Howe Cockerill, Esq., Commander, R. N. He sits in the House of Lords as Baron Ardrossan, and had the honour, on the meeting of the third session of the second Parliament of Victoria, February, 1843, of moving the address of the House of Lords on the speech of her most gracious Majesty.

ARMORIAL BEARINGS.

EARL OF EGLINTON :

> Quarterly: first and fourth az., three fleur de lis or, for Montgomery. Second and third gu., three rings or, gemmed az., for Eglinton. All within a bordure or, charged with a double tressure flory, counterflory gu., for Seton.
>
> CREST.—A female figure ppr., anciently attired az., holding in the dexter hand an anchor or, and in the sinister the head of a savage couped of the first.
>
> SUPPORTERS.—Two dragons vert, vomiting fire ppr.
>
> MOTTO.—" Gardez Bien."

No. 1.—LORD A. SEYMOUR :

> See those of Lady Seymour in Plate V.

No. 2.—F. CAVENDISH, ESQ. :

> Three stags heads cabossed ar.
>
> CREST.—On a ducal coronet a snake nowed, ppr.
>
> SUPPORTERS.—Two stags. The dexter, perfesse indented gules and sa. The sinister ppr. gorged with a chaplet of roses, alternately arg. and az., both attired and unguled, or.
>
> MOTTO.—" Cavendo tutus."

No. 3.—G. MAC DOUAL, ESQ. :

> Quarterly; first and fourth az., a lion rampant, ar. ; second and third, or, a lymphad sa., with a beacon on the topmast, ppr.
>
> CREST.—An arm in armour embowed fesseways, couped ppr., holding a cross crosslet fitchée.
>
> MOTTO.—" Vincam vel mori

LORD OF THE GOVERNMENT

Archibald William Montgomerie, Earl of Eglinton

PROCESSION TO THE LISTS. N°. 6.

J. Ford & Seymour.

Z.J. Cavenish, Esquire.

3. G. 6th Royal, Esquire.

DESCRIPTION OF PLATE—No. VII.

William, Earl of Craven . . . . **Knight of the Griffin.**

Henry de la Poer Beresford, Marquess of Waterford—Knight of the Dragon.

" Standards and gonfalons, 'twixt van and rear,
   Stream in the air."
                                        MILTON.

" Four knaves in garbs succinct, a trusty band,
   Caps on their heads, and halberds in their hand."
                                        POPE.

" Learned he was in medicinal lore,
   And by his side a pouch he wore."
                                        BUTLER.

" Holy Franciscan friar ! Brother ! ho !"
                                        SHAKSPEARE.

" Then, pilgrim, turn, thy cares forego ;
   All earthly cares are wrong ;
   Man wants but little here below,
   Nor wants that little long."
                                        GOLDSMITH.

" For I see, by thy bryght bassonet,
   Thow arte sum man of myght,
   And so I do by thy burnysshed brande,
   Thou art an yerle or ells a knyght."
                                        SONGE OF THE BATTELE OF OTTERBURNE.

HERE a group of the halberdiers of the Knight of the Griffin, William, Earl of Craven, take the lead : they are habited in the dress of retainers of the noble family to which they are attached, the colours of which were scarlet, white, and gold ; on their breasts is embroidered the crest of the Craven family—" a griffin statant, with wings elevated and endorsed of the last." The knight is on the war-horse which bore him gallantly in the Lists, and which was equipped in the protective armour of the age. He, himself, wears a splendid suit of engraved and gilt Milanese armour of the time of Henry the Eighth, and of the best form and workmanship. It was a fine example of the skill and taste displayed by the Italian armourers of the sixteenth century, and was purchased from the Marchese Tassoni D'ESTENSE. He is followed by his esquires, the Honourable F. Craven, and the Honourable J. Macdonald, who are in half-armour, with caps and plumes, the latter of the two bears the tilting helmet of the knight, which was remarkable for its elegance of contour and massive construction ; the cuisses and jambes were also of remarkable beauty. The banner is borne aloft by a man-at-arms. The next group is the halberdiers of the Knight of the Dragon—Henry de la Poer Beresford, Marquess of Waterford, in liveries of his colours, black and white, which were exceedingly picturesque and well chosen. One of them bears the tilting-shield. The Marquisate was created in 1789, and this nobleman is the third in descent, and sits in the House of Lords as Baron Tyrone, his second title being the Earl of Tyrone. His lordship has long been justly celebrated for his patronage and encouragement of all manly sports and amusements, and on this occasion contributed, by his strength, address, and activity, united with good humour, not only to uphold his high reputation, but to diffuse a universal good feeling and emulation among the combatants. On foot are seen Lord Ingestrie in the costume of an oriental physician. R. Mandeville, Esq., as a friar, with cross, belt, beads, &c., and C. Price, Esq., as a pilgrim from Palestine. Men-at-arms in coats of mail, on horseback, are clustered around them, one bearing the gonfalon. The Noble Marquess follows in a splendid suit of fluted armour of beautiful workmanship, of the early period of Richard the Third. The tilting helmet of this suit was of singularly fine workmanship, and characteristic of the same reign. The *manteau d'arme* is of considerable weight, it being absolutely necessary this piece should be of stout and sound material, to receive, without yielding, the powerful thrust of the tilting lance ; the steel-plated tilting saddle, together with the armour for the horse, were made for the occasion, from original models, it having been found impossible to find a sufficiency of ancient specimens for the occasion. The sword for the *meleé*, tilting lances, banners, &c., were all fine specimens of ancient weapons, and the whole of the appointments of the noble Marquess evinced the correct judgment of their owner in such formidable implements of warfare.

ARMORIAL BEARINGS.

Earl of Craven :

Quarterly : first and second.   A fesse between six crosses crosslet, fitchée gu., second and third or, five fleur de lis.

Crest.—On a chapeau purp. turned up ermine, a griffin sta., with wings elevated and endorsed of the last.

Supporters.—Two griffins.

Motto.—" Virtus in actione consistit."

Marquess of Waterford :

Ar., crusilly fitchee, sa., three fleur de lis within a bordure, engra, of the second.

Crest.—A dragon's head erased az., wounded with a broken spear through the neck or, the broken point ar., thrust through the upper jaw.

Supporters.—Two angels ppr.

Motto.—" Nil nisi cruce."

No. 1.—Hon. F. Craven :

A fesse between six crosslets, crosslet fitchée.

Crest.

Supporters.   } The same as the Earl of Craven.

Motto.

No. 2.—Hon. F. Macdonald :

Quarterly : first or, a lion rampant gu. ; second ar. a dexter hand couped, holding a cross crosslet fitchée sa. ; third ar. a lymphad ; fourth, a salmon swimming ppr.

Crest.—An arm armed gauntleted, holding a cross crosslet fitchée.

Supporters.—Two leopards ppr.

Motto.—" Nec tempore nec fato."

No. 3—Lord Ingestre :

Gules, a lion rampant with a bordure engrailed or.

Crest.—On a chapeau gu. turned up ermine, a lion statant or, the tail extended.

Supporters.—Two talbots gorged.

Motto.—" Humani nihil alienum."

No. 4.—R. Mandeville, Esq. :

Quarterly : or and gu.

No. 5.—C. Price, Esq. :

Or, a chevron erminos between three spear heads ar.

Crest.—A dragon's head vert, holding a hand in his mouth couped at the rest, dropping blood, all ppr.

KNIGHT OF WILLIAM. THE GRIFFIN. KNIGHT OF THE DRAGON.
EARL OF CRAVEN. HENRY DE LA POER BERESFORD
MARQUESS OF WATERFORD OF THE DRAGON.

1 Earl of Craven.   4 E. Mandeville, Esq.   5 C. Prior, Esq.
Hon. F. Fitzhardinge.   3 Lord Ingestrie.

PROCESSION TO THE LISTS. N.º 7.

DESCRIPTION OF PLATE—No. VIII.

Marquess of Waterford .... Continuation of Retinue.

John Hume Cust, Viscount Alford—Knight of the Black Lion.

" Your cavalcade the fair spectators view, From their standings, yet look up to you : From your brave train each singles out a ray, And longs to date a conquest from your day." <div align="right">DRYDEN.</div>	" Now thrive the armorers, and honours thought Reigns solely in the breast of every man." <div align="right">SHAKSPEARE.</div> " Well worthy be you of the armory, Wherein you have great glorry won this day." <div align="right">SPENCER, FAERY QUEEN.</div>

I N this throng are seen, first, the two pages, attendant upon the Marquess of Waterford—Lord John Beresford, and J. L. Ricardo, Esq., in helmets, back, and breast-plates of steel, arm-pieces, *garde de reins*, and buff boots; followed by the esquires, Sir Charles Kent and Mark Whyte, Esq. Men-at-arms in demi-suits of armour, on horseback, follow, one bearing the helmet, and another the banner. The halberdiers of the Knight of the Black Lion, John Hume Cust, Viscount Alford, in embroidered liveries of blue and white, are next in the procession. The gonfalon is borne by one of them. Men-at-arms, well mounted on war-horses, of great strength and noble action, follow; and then is seen the gallant knight himself, in a complete suit of polished steel plate armour, of the age of Henry the Eighth. The broad-toed solleret, and the general outline, are characteristic both of the date and country. His esquires, the Honourable Charles H. Cust, and Thomas Oliver Gascoigne, Esq., in half armour, with caps and plumes, are in attendance on him; one bears his banner, the other his tilting helmet, which is of great weight, and required considerable powers of endurance to wear it with the visor shut; the tilting pieces, saddle and horse armour, were of corresponding style and of great strength and temper. The emblazoned horse trappings of this knight were exceedingly splendid.

His lordship is the eldest son of the Earl of Brownlow, who is Lord Lieutenant, Custos Rotulorum and Vice Admiral of Lincolnshire.

On the upper border of the plate, Cupids support the armorial coats of the Marquess of Waterford and Viscount Alford; and the lower border contains those of the pages and esquires.

ARMORIAL BEARINGS.

VISCOUNT ALFORD :

Quarterly : first and fourth erm., on a chev. sa., three fountains ppr., for Cust; second or, an escutcheon between eight martlets in orle sa., for Brownlow; third, sa., a fesse erm. in chief, three crosses pattée fitchée ar., for Payne.

CREST.—A lion's head erased sa. gorged with a collar, paly wavy of six, ar. and az.

MOTTO.—" Opera Illius mea sunt."

No. 1.—LORD JOHN BERESFORD :

The same as those of the Marquess of Waterford, his brother.

No. 2.—J. L. RICARDO, ESQ. :

Gu., a bend varié, ar. and vert, between three garbs or, on a chief erm., a chessrook sa. between two bezants.

No. 3.—SIR CHARLES KENT, BART. :

Gu., three roses erm.

CREST.—A lion's head erased and collared.

No. 4.—MARK WHYTE, ESQ. :

Gu., on a canton ar., a lion rampant of the field, all within a bordure charged with eight estoilles of the second.

CREST.—An ostrich ar.

No. 5.—LORD MAIDSTONE :

Quarterly : first and fourth az., a chev. between three garbs or ; second and third ar., a chev. between three griffins pass., wings endorsed sa.

CREST.—A Pegasus courant ar., winged, manned, and hoofed or, ducally gorged of the last.

SUPPORTERS.—Dexter a Pegasus ar., wings, mane, and hoofs or, ducally gorged of the last, sinister a griffin, wings endorsed sa., ducally gorged or.

MOTTOES.—" Nil conscire sibi ;" and, " Virtus tutissima cassis."

No. 6.—HON. C. H. CUST.

The same as those of Viscount Alford, his brother.

No. 7.—T. O. GASCOIGNE, ESQ. :

Quarterly : first and fourth ar., pale sa., a demi-lucy, erect, couped or, a canton gu.; second and third ar., a chev. sa., between two pellets in chief, and a fish in base, gu.

CREST.—Out of a ducal coronet or ; a demi-lucy erect of the last charged with a pellet.

DESCRIPTION OF PLATE—No. IX.

George Augustus Frederick John Murray, Baron Glenlyon—
Knight of the Gael.

" It was a fair and gallant sight,
　To view them from the neighbouring height;
For strength and stature, from the clan,
Each warrior was a chosen man:
As even afar might well be seen,
By their proud step and martial mien;
　Their feathers dance, their tartans float,
　Their targets gleam.
A wild and warlike group they stand,
That well became such mountain strand.

The warriors left their lowly bed,
Look'd out upon the dappled sky,
Muttered their soldier matins by,
And then awaked their fire, to steal,
As short and rude, their soldier meal.

That o'er, the Gael around him threw
His graceful plaid of varied hue,
And, true to promise, led the way
By thicket green, and mountain grey.
So tangled oft, that, bursting through,
Each hawthorn shed her showers of dew,
That diamond dew, so pure and clear,
It rivals all but beauty's tear!"

SCOTT.

" So may, through Albion's farthest ken,
To social-flowing glasses,
The grace be—Athole's honest men,
And Athole's bonnie lasses."

BURNS.

JUSTICE can scarcely be done to this part of the procession by any description or illustration. In it George Murray, Baron Glenlyon, Knight of the Gael, is represented in a suit of polished steel-plate armour, attended by his esquires, Sir David Dundas, Baronet, and John Balfour, Esquire, and surrounded by a strong guard of hardy Highlanders. These Highlanders, all retainers and tenants of the "Athole," marched from their native hills to Eglinton, under the command of the Honourable James Plantaganet Murray, John Murray Drummond, Esq., and Charles Home Drummond, Esq., most excellent portraits of whom, in their full national costume, are here given.

They entered the park on the evening immediately preceding the commencement of the Tournament. In number they must have amounted to nearly a hundred and fifty, all picked men, in the costume and tartan of the Clan Murray, armed with broad-sword or claymore, and target, dirk, and pistol. Their approach was announced by the sound of the bagpipes, the pipers striking up the tune peculiar to the clan, which, re-echoed by the woods and hills, rang loudly, yet melodiously, throughout the whole district, and brought hundreds to witness their arrival. They were immediately drawn up in front of the Castle, and in the course of the evening, went through the manœuvres by which the Highland clans are distinguished from more regular troops, and shewed that, in the management of their weapons, they had in no wise lost the skill of their celebrated ancestors, or deteriorated from the martial spirit and discipline of the "Gael." This display formed one of the most distinguished episodes in the warlike games at the Castle; and on the following day these brave mountaineers escorted their Knight to the Lists, as is here represented. His lordship, one of the most accomplished noblemen on the ground, was armed *cap à pie* in a suit of polished plate armour, of the time of Henry the Eighth, with skirt of chain mail. The tilting apparel was in keeping, consisting of the emblazoned *manteau d'arme*, the *mentoniere*, the bridle gauntlet, and the tilting lance with van plate. The horse was defended by the manefure and chanfron, and had the tilting saddle with steel-plates. The gonfalon and banner were each borne by a man-at-arms. Altogether, the Knight of the Gael and his retinue, in liveries of green, blue, and crimson, were one of the most characteristic features of this splendid procession.

His lordship is heir presumptive to the dukedom of Atholé, being the nephew of the present duke, who is unmarried. The second title of this illustrious family is Marquess of Tullèbardine, and the office of sheriff of Perthshire is hereditary in it. On the late occasion of her Majesty's visit to Scotland, she was met, in her progress from Perth to Taymouth Castle, by the noble Baron, at the head of the same gallant body of Highlanders, with whose martial appearance her Majesty, and her illustrious consort Prince Albert, were pleased to express their high gratification.

In the upper border, Cupids are represented with bunches of the juniper plant. The juniper is introduced because it is a badge of the noble house to which this Baron belongs. The heraldic coat of his lordship is in the centre. On the lower border are those of the above-named gentlemen commanding the Highlanders, and also those of Sir David Dundas, Baronet, and John Balfour, Esq., the esquires.

ARMORIAL BEARINGS.

BARON GLENLYON:

Quarterly: first az., three mullets ar., within a double tressure, flory counterflory or, for Murray; second, gu., three legs in armour ppr., garnished and spurred or, conjoined in triangle at the upper part of the thigh; third, quarterly, first, and fourth ar., on a bend az., three stags' heads cabossed or, second and third gu., two lions passant, on pale ar.; fourth, quarterly, first and fourth or, a fesse chequy ar. and az., second and third, paly of six or, and sa.

CREST.—A demi-savage ppr., wreathed about the head and waist vert, holding in the dexter hand a dagger, also ppr., pomel and hilt or, and in the sinister a key of the last vert.

MOTTO.—" Furth Fortune and fill the fetters."

No. 1.—JOHN BALFOUR, ESQ., of Balbirnie:

Ar, a chevron between three otters heads erased sa.

CREST.—A palm tree ppr.

MOTTO.—" Virtus ad æthera tendit."

No. 2.—SIR DAVID DUNDAS, BART., of Dunira:

Ar, a lion rampant gu., within a bordure ermine.

CREST.—A lion's face in a bush ppr.

MOTTO.—" Essayez."

No. 3.—HONOURABLE JAMES PLANTAGANET MURRAY:

The same as those of Baron Glenlyon.

No. 4.—JOHN MURRAY DRUMMOND, ESQ.:

Per fesse wavy or, and gules.

CREST.—Two arms in the act of drawing a bow and arrow ppr.

MOTTO.—" Marte et arte."

No. 5.—JAMES HOME DRUMMOND, ESQ.:

Quarterly: first and fourth or, three bars wavy, gu., within a bordure az.; second and third quarterly, first and second a lion rampant, second three popingays vert; third, three shields, third quarterly, first a lion rampant, second three popingays vert; third, hunting horns stringed gu.; fourth gu., a pelican.

CREST.—A lion rampant, az.

MOTTO.—" Dum spiro spero."

THE KNIGHT OF GAEL

GEORGE AUGUSTUS FREDERICK JOHN MURRAY, BARON GLENLYON

DESCRIPTION OF PLATE—No. X.

Archibald, Earl of Cassilis . . . . Knight of the Dolphin.

The Honourable Henry Hall Gage—Knight of the Ram.

<table>
<tr><td>

" Heaven in thy good cause make thee prosperous !
Be swift like lightning in the execution,
And let thy blows, doubly redoubled,
Fall like amazing thunder on the casque
Of thy adverse pernicious enemy :
Rouse up thy youthful blood,
Be valiant and live."
SHAKSPEARE.

</td><td>

" A radiant baldric, o'er his shoulder ty'd,
Sustain'd the sword that glitter'd at his side :
His youthful face a polish'd helm o'erspread,
The waving horsehair nodded on his head,
His figured shield, a shining orb, he takes,
And in his hand a pointed jav'lin shakes."
ILIAD.

</td></tr>
</table>

 NIGHTLY retainers of the Knight of the Dolphin are seen on the left, the gonfalon being borne by a stalwart man-at-arms on horseback, in complete armour. The banner and helmet are borne by attendants on foot. The Knight of the Dolphin, Archibald, Earl of Cassilis, follows, sheathed from head to foot in a splendid suit of steel armour, of rich Spanish workmanship, engraved and gilt. It was profusely covered with engravings in design of trophies of arms, &c., and from the frequent repetition of the monogram, C.M., is supposed to have been made for one of the Medina family, about the reign of Philip II. The suit has the chain mail skirt. The tilting apparel of the noble earl was of fine character ; the *manteau d'arme* and *mentorie*, the bridle, gauntlet, &c., being *en suite*. The *chanfron* and *manefure* were also gilt. The caparisons were in colours—scarlet, black, and white—richly emblazoned with the armorial bearings of the rider. The whole had an appearance of dignity and splendour, corresponding with the exalted rank of the "belted earl," and was much admired.

His lordship is grandson of the Marquess of Ailsa.

The halberdiers of the Knight of the Ram immediately follow the Earl of Cassilis, one of them carrying the gonfalon of his master.

The Knight of the Ram, the Honourable Henry Hall Gage, is next in the procession. He wears a *cap à pie* suit of polished plate armour, of the date of Elizabeth, brought from the armoury at Santarem, with skirt of chain mail ; the tilting apparel, viz., the *mentorie, manteau d'arme*, and bridle gauntlet, emblazoned with heraldic bearings *en suite*. The horse was also armed with *manefure* and *chanfron*. The colours of the honourable knight were blue, white, and crimson.

The Hon. Captain Gage is the son of Viscount Gage who sits in Parliament as Baron Gage. His esquires, on horseback, R. Murray, Esq., carrying the helmet, and R. Fergusson, Esq., bearing the banner, concludes this plate.

The upper border represents Cupids with fruits and garlands of flowers, supporting the armorial coats of the two knights, and on the lower one are those of the esquires.

ARMORIAL BEARINGS.

THE EARL OF CASSILIS :

   Ar. a chev. gu. between three crosses crosslet fitcheé sa., within a double tressure, flory, counterflory, of the second.
   CREST.—A dolphin naiant ppr.
   MOTTO.—"Avise la fin."

THE HON. HENRY HALL GAGE :

   Quarterly : first and fourth, per saltire az. and ar., a saltire gu. ; second and third az. The sun in splendour or.
   CREST.—A ram pass. ar., armed and enguled or.
   MOTTO.—"Courage sans peur."

No. 1.—R. MURRAY, ESQ. :

   Quarterly : first and fourth az., three stars within a double tressure, flory, counterflory, with fleur de lis or, for Murray ; second and third gu. ; three crosses
      pattee or, for Barclay of Balvaird.
   CREST.—A buck's head couped ppr., between the antlers a cross pattée ar.
   SUPPORTERS.—Two lions gu., armed or
   MOTTOES.—"Spero meliora ;" and, "Uni æquus virtuti."

No. 2.—R. FERGUSSON, ESQ. :

   Az., a buckle ar., between three boars erased or.
   CREST.—An arm in armour grasping a broken spear, all proper.
   MOTTO.—"True to the last."

KNIGHT OF THE RAM.

HONOURABLE HENRY BALL G. &c. OF KNIGHT.

DOLPHIN. KNIGHT OF CASSILLIS.

ARCHIBALD KENNEDY. EARL

DESCRIPTION OF PLATE—No. XI.

Walter Little Gilmour, Esq. . . . . The Black Knight.

The Honorable Edward Stafford Jerningham—The Knight of the Swan.

" His acton it was all of blacke,
　His hewberke and his sheelde,
Ne noe man wist whence he did come,
Ne noe man knew where he did gone,
　When they came from the feelde :
Then forthe the stranger knight he came
　In his black armoure dight."
　　　　　M.S. IN BISHOP PERCY'S COLLECTION.

" Paregall to dukes, with kings he might compare,
　Surmountinge in honor all erls he did excede,
To all cuntries aboute him reporte me I dare,
　Lyke to Eneas benygne in worde and dede,
　Valiaunt as Hector in every marciall nede,
　Provydent, discrete, circumspect, and wyse,
Tyll the chaunce ran agyne him of fortune's duble dyse."
　　　　　JOHN SHELTON.

EADING the way the retainers of the Black Knight, bearing his gonfalon and shield, come first. The Black Knight himself, in a *cap à pie* suit of black armour of the date of Henry the Eighth, and brought from the royal armoury at Santarem, is then seen on a spirited black charger, with sable caparisons. He is unattended by any esquires, and his gonfalon, banner, and shield are without devices. The banner is borne by Lord Drumlanrig, and the helmet by Captain Blair.

John Campbell, Esq., of Saddell, was to have personified the Black Knight, but not being sufficiently recovered from the injury received while tilting at the Eyre Arms, Walter Little Gilmour, Esq., of Inch, near Edinburgh, took his place in the Tournament, and most efficiently supported the character. The sombre appearance of his colours formed a remarkable contrast with the splendid trappings and housings of the rest of the cavalcade, producing, by that very contrast, the most striking and happy effect.

Next in the programme are two men-at-arms in half armour, one of whom bears the gonfalon of the Knight of the Swan, the Honourable Edward Stafford Jerningham, who is then seen in a suit of polished steel *cap à pie* armour, of the date of Henry the Eighth, from the royal collection of Portugal. It is worthy of note that the only piece of armour that yielded to the powerful blows dealt with the heavy swords used in the *mêlée*, was the right hand gauntlet of this suit, which was cut through the inner and thinner plate. He wears a skirt of chain mail. An attendant on foot carries the shield. The esquires, Garden Campbell, Esq., and Captain Stephenson, follow on horseback, the one bearing the emblazoned banner of the knight, and the other his tilting helmet, surmounted with crest and plume.

The horse armour and caparisons consist of the chanfron and manefure and the steel plated saddle. The housings, emblazoned with heraldic devices, and the colours of his liveries, were crimson and white.

The Honourable Edward Stafford Jerningham is the eldest son of Lord Stafford.

ARMORIAL BEARINGS.

WALTER LITTLE GILMOUR, ESQ.:

　Quarterly : first and fourth az., a car between three fleur-de-lis in chief, or, and a pen in base ar.; second sa., on a saltire ar., a crescent of the first ; third, gu., three boars' heads erased ar., in each flank, or Lochaber axe of the last.

　CREST.—A hand holding a garland of laurel ppr.

　SUPPORTERS.—Two hawks rising ppr.

　MOTTO.—" Perseveranti dabitur."

HON. EDWARD STAFFORD JERNINGHAM :

　Three lozenge-shaped arming buckles gu., tongues fesseways.

　CREST.—A stag lodged ppr.

　MOTTO.—" Amo probos."

No. 1.—CAPTAIN BLAIR :

　Quarterly : first and fourth, ar., a chevron between three hunting horns ; second and third, on a saltire sa., nine mascles of the first, in chief an estoille gu.

No. 2.—LORD DRUMLANRIG :

　Quarterly : first and fourth ar., a human heart gu., imperially crowned, ppr., on a chief az., three mullets of the field ; second and third az., a bend between six crosses crosslet fitchée or, all within a bordure of the last, charged with the double tressure of Scotland.

　CREST.—A man's heart gu., with an imperial crown and winged or.

　SUPPORTERS.—A pegasus on each side.

　MOTTO.—" Forward."

No. 3.—CAPTAIN STEPHENSON :

　Ar., a chevron between three fleur az. on a chief of the last, as many mullets of the first.

　CREST.—A hand holding a laurel garland, all ppr.

　MOTTO.—" Cœlum non solum."

No. 4.—GARDEN CAMPBELL, ESQ. :

　Quarterly : first and third, quarterly, first and fourth, a gyronny of eight ; second and third, a stag's head ppr., an escutcheon pendent ; first and third, two boars erased for Garden ; second and fourth, quarterly, first and third a roundle ; second and third quarterly ; first and second a chevron between three stars, second and third per fesse.

　CREST.—An eagle with two heads rising from the flames.

　MOTTO.—" I bide my time."

THE EGLINTON TOVRNAMENT.

PROCESSION TO THE LISTS—CONTINUED.

DESCRIPTION OF PLATE—No. XII.

James Ogilvie Fairlie, Esq.—Knight of the Golden Lion.

"As when a lion in his den
　Hath heard the hunter's cries,
And rushes forth to meet his foes;
　So did the knight arise."
　　　　THE HERMIT OF WARKWORTH.

"A helmett of proofe hee strait did provide,
　A strong arminge sworde hee girt by his side,
On his hand a goodly faire gauntlett put hee;
Was not this a brave knight, Captain Fairlie?"
　　　ANCIENT BALLAD IN THE PEPY'S COLLECTION.

"To fight with him I saw noe cause,
　Me thought it was not meet;

For he was stiffe and strong with all,
　His strokes were nothing sweete."
　　　　THE MARRIAGE OF SIR GAWAINE.

"Of Hawkyn, of Herry,
　Of Tomkyn, of Terry,
Of them that were doughty
And stalworth in dede."
　　　　THE TOURNAMENT OF TOTTENHAM.

"Turn'd on the horse his armed heel,
　And stirr'd his courage with the steel,
Bounded the fiery steed in air,
The rider sat erect and fair."
　　　　SIR WALTER SCOTT.

MARSHALLED in rank, the retinue of the Knight of the Golden Lion occupy the left side of the Plate. The gonfalon floats bravely to the breeze in proud defiance. Halberdiers are clustered around, followed by those formidable men-at-arms on horseback, by whose strength, discipline, and valour, the battles of former days were in general decided.

The Knight of the Golden Lion, James Ogilvie Fairlie, Esq., is then seen, mounted on one of the most noble horses which appeared in the Tournament, caparizoned in colours, blue and crimson, and emblazoned with the heraldic bearings of his rider. The *chanfron* and *manefure*, gilt *en suite*, and the tilting-saddle, with steel-plates, were all of the finest workmanship.

The Knight himself was cased from head to heel in a suit of beautifully polished plate armour, remarkable for its elegant form, and of the date of Henry the Eighth, richly gilt, and emblazoned with the arms and crest of the Knight.

James Ogilvie Fairlie, Esq., of Williamfield, in the county of Ayr, is the son of W. M. Fairlie, Esq., late of Calcutta. His bearing was truly noble, and he acquitted himself, on this occasion, in a manner that did high honour to these noble sports.

His standard-bearer, Charles Cox, Esq., wears a suit of steel armour, gilt; and his esquires, Captain Pettat and Captain Purves, follow next, one bearing his helmet, deserving of particular notice for its most knightly contour.

Cupids, enwreathed in flowers, form the border, in the upper part of which is the heraldic coat of the Knight, and on the lower one those of his attendants.

ARMORIAL BEARINGS.

JAMES OGILVIE FAIRLIE, ESQ.:
　Or, a lion rampant, and in chief three stars gu.
　CREST.—A lion's head couped or.
　MOTTO.—"Paratus sum."

No. 1.—CHARLES COX, ESQ.:
　Sa., a chevron between three stags' heads cabossed.
　CREST.—A stag levant, regard. ar.

No. 2.—CAPTAIN PURVES:
　Az. on a fesse between three mascles ar. as many cinque-foils of the first.
　CREST.—The sun rising out of a cloud ppr.
　MOTTO.—"Clarior e tenebris."

No. 3.—CAPTAIN PETTAT:
　Gu., a chevron between three wolves' heads ar.

KNIGHTS OF THE GOLDEN LION

SIEGE OF CALAIS

JAMES OGILVIE FAIRLIE ESQ.

PROCESSION TO THE LISTS—CONTINUED.

DESCRIPTION OF PLATE—No. XIII.

Charles Lamb, Esq.—Knight of the White Rose.

" Then will I lift aloft the milk white rose,
    With whose sweet smell the air shall be perfumed ;
    And in my standard bear the arms of York."

" A son, who is the theme of Honour's tongue ;
    Amongst a grove, the very straitest plant,
    Who is sweet Fortune's minion, and her pride."

" Speak terms of manage to thy bounding steed ;
    Cry courage !—to the field !"

" So shall inferior eyes,
    That borrow their behaviours from the great,
    Grow great by your example, and put on
    The dauntless spirit of resolution.

Away, and glister like the god of war,
    When he intendeth to become the field :
    Shew boldness, and aspiring confidence."

SHAKSPEARE.

NOTHING could exceed the chaste and elegant costumes of the retinue of Charles Lamb, Esq., the accomplished and gallant Knight of the White Rose; the colours of which were blue and gold, trimmed with white swan's-down fur, and, as represented in this plate, formed a light and most beautiful contrast with the gorgeous colours which, on all hands, presented themselves to the eyes of the spectators. First in the procession is seen Robert Crawfurd, Esq., who bears aloft the banner of his knight. Then comes the gallant knight himself who wears a suit of polished steel *cap à pie* armour of early form, with a skirt of chain mail. It will be observed that the tilting-shield, borne by one of the esquires, is of a different form and material to those worn by other knights, the one here represented is of wood, covered with a thin plate of steel, and was constructed under the direction of the knight himself, but from its insufficiency to resist the thrust of the lance had nearly proved fatal to him in the passage of arms subsequently held at Irvine. It was emblazoned with a White Rose, and the motto—" Une seule." The helmet, which is remarkable for its fine character, is surmounted with the crest and plume of the knight, and borne by another of his esquires. The *mentoniere*, bridle gauntlet, van plate, *chanfron*, and *manefure*, were all in keeping with the fine suit worn by this knight, and proved his good taste and correct judgment in the choice of his arms and armour. A body of archers, on foot, commanded by Patrick Gordon, Esq., take up the remainder of this Plate. They formed a body-guard, escorting their knight to the Lists, and added much to the beauty of the procession by their gay, yet martial appearance.

Charles Lamb, Esq., is the eldest son of Sir Charles Montolieu Lamb, Baronet, and half brother to the Earl of Eglinton. When in the Lists the manly bearing and elegant appointments of the Knight of the White Rose, elicited the most marked approbation, and were the theme of conversation to all who had a taste for the martial costumes of the middle ages.

The upper border is formed of Cupids, with wreaths encircling the arms of the knight, and in the lower border are those of his attendants, with Cupids and bows, arrows, and targets.

ARMORIAL BEARINGS.

CHARLES LAMB, ESQ. :
    Ar., a fesse lozenge or, and az. in chief, three mascles of the third base fusily, within a bordure of the same bezantée.
    CREST.—A camel's head proper, erased gu.
    MOTTO.—" Deo et Principe."
NO. 1.—R. CRAWFURD, ESQ. :
    A gyrony of eight ; first quarter, a gyrony of eight.

KNIGHT OF THE "WHITE ROSE."

CHARLES LAMB, ESQUIRE.

PROCESSION TO THE LISTS. N°.IX.

DESCRIPTION OF PLATE—No. XIV.

Sir Francis Hopkins, Baronet—Knight of the Burning Tower.

Richard Lechmere, Esq. . . . . . . Knight of the Red Rose.

"Born of noble state,
Well could he tourney, and in Lists debate."
SPENSER.

"He lived with all the pomp he could devise,
At tilts and tournaments obtain'd the prize."

"The following cavalcade, by three and three,
Proceed by titles marshall'd in degree."
DRYDEN.

"Onward they press, where glory calls, to arms,
And spring to war from Pleasure's silken charms;
THE HENRIADE.

"In what martial equipage
They issue forth, steel bows, and shafts their arms,
Of equal dread in flight, or in pursuit;
All horsemen, in which fight they most excel;
See how in warlike muster they appear."
MILTON.

"All brave in arms well train'd to wield
The heavy halbert, brand, and shield:
And now by holytide and feast,
From rules of discipline released."
SCOTT.

N the left of the Plate is seen the gonfalon of Sir Francis Hopkins, Bart., Knight of the Burning Tower, borne by a man-at-arms on foot, in the armour of the infantry of the sixteenth century. He is followed by retainers on foot, one of whom bears the banneret, and the other the tilting-helmet.

The gallant Knight himself is then seen, mounted on a noble charger, and encased in a *cap à pie* suit of polished steel armour, of very exquisite workmanship, of the date of Henry the Eighth, furnished with a skirt of chain mail. The fine-marked and peculiar character of this suit was much admired. The helmet, borne by an attendant, was surmounted with the crest of the Knight. The whole of the tilting apparel was in correct taste, emblazoned with heraldic bearings, and comprised the *mentoniere*, the *manteau d'arme*, bridle gauntlet, tilting lance, and van plate. The horse armour was also very elaborate, consisting of the *manefure, chanfron*, and the tilting saddle, with steel plates and gilt stirrups. The caparisons and liveries, in colours of black and gold, had a very imposing and grand effect.

Sir Francis Hopkins, of Athboy, in the county of Meath, was born in 1813, and succeeded to the title in 1814. The baronetcy was created in 1795.

Immediately following is the *cortège* of the Knight of the Red Rose, or Rose of Lancaster, Richard Lechmere, Esq. A man in armour on foot bearing the gonfalon, and accompanied by a monk with a cross, is first seen, and then comes the gallant Knight himself wearing a beautiful suit of polished steel german-fluted armour. This suit was of grand proportions and elaborate workmanship, and is of the era of the Emperor Maximilian. The horse of the Knight was an animal of remarkable strength and beauty, and is attended by grooms.

The esquires, J. C. Corry, Esq., and Corbet Smith, Esq., follow on horseback, one bearing the banner and the other the tilting helmet of their Knight. The tilting apparel and horse-armour were of the same complete character as described above, and the caparisons and liveries were in colours of scarlet and white.

This Knight is understood to have assumed the badge of the Red Rose in right of pure descent from the House of Lancaster, and the armorial bearings of his family are among the earliest registered in the Heralds' Collection.

The knights visitors in ancient costumes, whose names are given in the Official Programme, followed by the officers of the Castle, the Seneschal and Chamberlain of the household, closed the procession of the knights to the Lists, and formed, as a whole, the most magnificent pageant on record.

ARMORIAL BEARINGS.

SIR FRANCIS HOPKINS, BART.:
Sa. on a chev. between three dexter gauntlets or, as many roses gu., seeded and barbed vert.
CREST.—A tower ar., fired ppr.
MOTTO.—"Aut suavitate aut vi."

RICHARD LECHMERE, ESQ.:
Gu., a fess or, and two pelicans in chief arg.
CREST.—Out of a ducal coronet a pelican or, vulning itself ppr.
MOTTO.—"Ducit amor patriæ."

No. 1.—J. C. CORRY, ESQ.:
Gu., a saltire argent, and a rose or.
CREST.—A cock ppr.

No. 2.—CORBET SMITH, ESQ.:
Sa. on a chevron between three roses.

KNIGHTS OF THE BURNING TOWER. KNIGHTS OF THE RED ROSE.

SIR FRANCIS HOPKINS, BART.

RICHARD LECHMERE, ESQ.

DESCRIPTION OF PLATE—No. XV.

The General View of the Lists.

" The ladies dress'd in rich cymars were seen,
Of Florence satin, flower'd with white and green,
And for a shade betwixt the bloomy gridelin;
The borders of their petticoats below,
Were guarded thick with rubies on a row;
And every damsel wore upon her head,
Of flowers a garland, blended white and red.
Attired in mantles all the knights were seen,
That gratified the view with cheerful green;
Their chaplets, of the ladies' colours, were
Composed of white and red, to shade their shining hair.
Before the merry troop the minstrels play'd;
All in their master's liveries were array'd.
Their instruments were various in their kind,
Some for the bow, snd some for breathing wind:
The sawtry, pipe, and hautboy, noisy band,
And the soft lute trembling beneath the touching hand."
CHAUCER, THE FLOWER AND THE LEAF.

" The trumpets sound—
And warlike symphony is heard around."

" Next these the kindred of the knights are graced
With nearer seats, and lords by ladies placed;
Scarce were they seated, when, with clamours loud,
In rush'd at once a rude promiscuous crowd:
The guards, and these each other overbear,
And in a moment throng the spacious theatre;
Now changed the jarring noise to whispers low,
As winds forsaking seas more softly blow."

" Thus ranged the herald for the last proclaims,
A silence while they answer'd to their names."
CHAUCER.

PERSONS who had the good fortune to be present at the celebration of this grand spectacle, will recognise, at a glance, the correctness and fidelity of this representation of the "Lists." The tilting ground was chosen with excellent judgment by the noble Earl of Eglinton. It was marked out in a part of the elegant domain in the park of the Castle which was bounded on one side by a gentle slope, on which the great masses of spectators, certainly not less in number than sixty thousand took their position, and from which the whole were enabled, without difficulty, to view, as from an eminence, all that was going on in the plain beneath them; opposite to this slope, on the other side of the plain, was erected the grand balcony, in which was placed the throne of the Queen of Beauty, the seats of her attendants, and the seats and places set apart for the numerous, illustrious, and eminent personages who honoured the sports by their presence. There were also other balconies on this side of the Lists, and the whole afforded accommodation for several thousands of visitors. The tilting ground itself, was a fine plain of verdant turf, perfectly flat, and admirably adapted to the purposes to which it was put. At either end were seen the magnificent pavilions of the knights about to engage in the warlike contests, and the outside covering of the pavilions being in stripes of the colours of the respective knights, added much to the general effect and beauty of the scene. They were also decorated with armorial bearings; emblazoned shields were affixed to the sides of their entrances, and banners, pennons, and flags, rustled bravely in the wind from their summits. Here were to be seen, bands of retainers, servitors, grooms, and attendants; some in busy preparation, examining the lances of the knights, arranging pieces of armour, attending to the wants of the numerous war-horses, which neighed in proud defiance of each other. Here, too, were to be seen those temporary idlers whose hour for active service had not yet arrived, carousing from the wine cup, the rich fluids, which were with a most liberal hand supplied by knightly munificence, as in the best days of chivalry and hospitality. The scene was at once imposing from its magnificence, and jocund from its good humour. It was diversified most strongly, yet most pleasingly, by the variety of costume, the brilliancy of colour, and the quaintness of character in many of the habiliments of the many thousands habited in ancient fashions. Strong bodies of men-at-arms were passing and repassing continually, yet no disorder was observable, so excellent were the arrangements of the Knight Marshal of the Lists, and so well did his subordinates, the Deputy Marshals, carry his orders into effect. Along the plain, midway between the slope before-mentioned and the grand balcony, ran the barrier (as seen in the representation). It extended in length 300 yards, was five feet and a half high, built of strong planks, supported by pallisades, precisely according to the laws of chivalry in the middle ages; along the sides of the barrier, the turf was thickly strewn with sawdust, to prevent the horses from slipping. The Lists themselves, which occupied rather more than three acres of ground, were surrounded by a strong fence of pallisades, to prevent the promiscuous intrusion of too large a crowd, and the possibility of accidents.

As it is important that all that can illustrate this portion of the Tournament be understood, we may be pardoned for extracting a part of the description of the Lists from an account published at the time, at Edinburgh, which is accurately correct.

"At the south end of the Lists, on either side of the entrance, stood the tent and pavilions of the Earl of Eglinton, azure and or. Immediately on the right stood the pavilion of Lord George Beresford, sable and argent; also on the south side of the Lists, and on the other side of Lord Eglinton's encampment, stood the pavilion of Mr. Jerningham, gules and argent. Lord Glenlyon's tent and pavilions, azure, gules, and vert, were erected on the east side of the Lists, immediately beside Lord George Beresford's; and Mr. Lechmere's appeared next in order, with the pavilion of the Black Knight, sable, on the right. At the northen end of the Lists, Earl Craven's tent and pavilions, gules and argent, occupied the centre, with Captain Fairlie's, gules and azure; Mr. Lamb's, azure and or lozenge, over argent; the Earl of Cassilis, Captain Gage's, and Sir Francis Hopkins', argent, extending towards the east; and with Viscount Alford's, azure and argent; and the Marquess of Waterford's, argent and sable, towards the west. Of the galleries with which the eastern side of the Lists was occupied, the central one was fitted up with great magnificence, and built in the Gothic style of architecture. The throne for the Queen of Beauty formed a part of the grand gallery, which, at this point, slightly jutting out, at once caught the eye, not less from its prominence than from the elaborate carved work overlaid with gold, which surmounted this regal seat, and from the drapery of crimson damask with which it was hung. The smaller galleries were also richly ornamented. The grand gallery accommodated 800 persons, and, in the lower part of it, seats were provided for the Eglinton tenantry; while the galleries by which it was flanked held 600 each."

This will convey some notion of the general magnificence of the scene, which was rendered still more exciting from the bustle and animation which pervaded every part, the careering of the steeds, the tumult of preparation for the joust, the shouts of the spectators, and the eager expectation of the vast multitude.

The border or frame of this plate describes recumbent figures of warriors.

GENERAL VIEW OF THE CAMP

PROCESSION TO THE LISTS—CONTINUED.

DESCRIPTION OF PLATE—No. XVI.

The Challenge.

" *Dieu de* batailles ! where have they this mettle ?
Is not their climate foggy, raw, and dull ;
On whom, as in despight, the sun looks pale,
Killing their fruit with frowns ?   Can sodden water,
A drench for sur-reyn'd jades, their barley broth
Decoct their cold blood to such valiant heat ?"

    " Then let the trumpets sound
The tucket-sonuance, and the note to mount."

" Marshal, ask yonder knight in arms,
Both who he is, and why he cometh hither
Thus plated in habiliments of war ;

And formally according to our law
Depose him in the justice of his cause."

    " My dancing soul doth celebrate
This feast of battle with mine adversary."

" Being mounted and both roused in their seats,
Their neighing coursers daring of the spur,
Their armed staves in charge, their beavers down,
Their eyes of fire sparkling through sights of steel,
And the loud trumpet blowing them together."

        SHAKSPEARE.

RIGIDLY adhering to the feats of the Tournament, the artist has here represented the " Challenge."   In the back ground are seen the trees and the spectators, and in the middle distance the pavilions.

The halberdiers are at their posts, whilst an esquire to the Earl of Eglinton holds a gauntlet.   The friar is happily introduced; should either knight be mortally wounded, the office of this " holy man" would be in immediate requisition, and though, fortunately, such was not here the case, his presence was necessary to make the representation perfect, and is in strict accordance with the custom of the middle ages. The figure in half-armour, on foot, is Lord Maidstone. In the middle of the picture is the Marquess of Waterford, whose horse is rearing.   He accepts the challenge to meet the Lord of the Tournament in the Lists.   One of the esquires of the noble Marquess prepares to give him his lance.   An armourer is properly introduced ; another esquire is in the act of mounting. This Plate is an exact representation of this most interesting moment.   The eyes of the concourse of spectators were bent upon the scene with an intensity of feeling which it is impossible adequately to describe, and all was hushed in silence as the challenge was given and received.

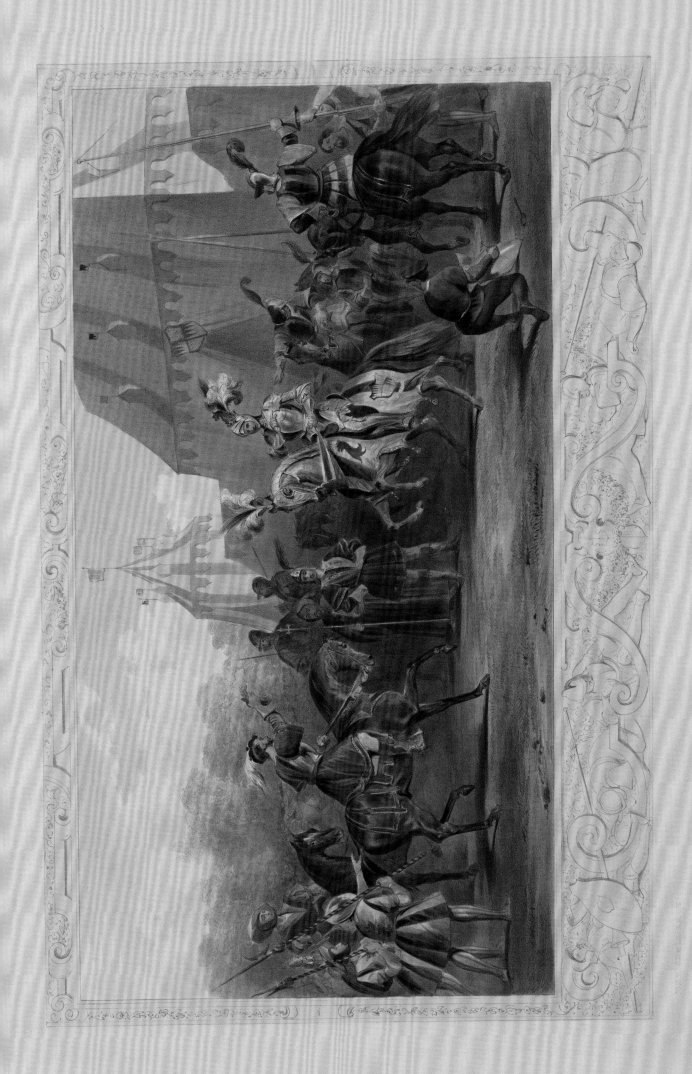

THE EGLINTON TOURNAMENT.

DESCRIPTION OF PLATE—No. XVII.

The Joust.

" Be stirring as the time; be fire with fire;
    Threaten the threatener, and outface the brow
    Of bragging horror: so shall inferior eyes,
    That borrow their behaviour from the great,
    Grow great by your example, and put on
    The dauntless spirit of resolution.
    Away; and glister like the God of war,
    When he intendeth to become the field:
    Shew boldness and aspiring confidence.

"———— By that sword I swear,
    Which gently laid my knighthood on my shoulder,
    I'll answer thee in any fair degree,
    Or chivalrous design of knightly trial:
    And, when I mount, alive may I not light,
    If I be traitor, or unjustly fight!"
                      SHAKSPEARE.

"———— you shall see
    Justice decide the victor's chivalry.
    Lord Marshal, command our officer at arms
    Be ready to direct these home alarms.

" This is the day appointed for the combat;
    And ready are the appellant and defendant.
    The armourer and his man, to enter the lists,
    So please your lordship to behold the fight."
                      SHAKSPEARE.

" He that bear'th him best in the Tournament,
    Shal be granted the Gree by the common assent."
             TOURNAMENT OF TOTTENHAM.

" A steed in haste ful knightly he bestrode
    And them amonge like Mars himself he rode."
            LYDGATE's " BOKE OF TROY."

 ELDOM has such a scene as this Plate presents been viewed in the annals of the best days of chivalry. Before describing the Plate, it will be necessary to give an account of the Jousts generally, and we will avail ourselves of an extract from the publication before quoted as being germane to the purpose.

" The Irvine archers, clad in Lincoln green, took their station in a line in front of the grand gallery; and the sturdy followers of Lord Glenlyon, to the number of a hundred, all arrayed in the Highland garb of Atholé tartan, remained on the opposite side of the Lists. The ground was kept by a party of the Ayrshire yeomanry.

" When the Lord of the Tournament, the Earl of Eglinton, proceeded with head unhelmed to pay his devoirs to the Queen of Beauty, shouts of applause burst from every side; and the woods re-echoed the plaudits which were repeated as he gracefully bowed to the noble and fair occupants of the grand gallery.

" The lances of the knights, which were arranged in conical form, on stands at either end of the Lists, were about twice the length of the combatants, and were headed with rochets, or round flat pieces of wood, as ' the arms of courtesy' were wont to be. It may also be premised that, in tilting, the combatants first proceed to the opposite ends of the barrier, parallel with which they are then to gallop, the one on the one side and the other on the other, holding their spears inclined, with the points across the barrier, until meeting in mid career, they do honour to themselves by breaking their lance on the defensive armour of their adversary.

" The Knight of the Swan, was the first knight who appeared for the purpose of tilting. He was opposed by the Knight of the Golden Lion. In the first course they passed without touching, and the course was not reckoned; the masque of iron on the horse of the Knight of the Swan was loosened in the second; in the third his horse swerved from the barrier; but in the fourth the Knight of the Golden Lion broke his lance on the shield of his opponent.

" The Earl of Eglinton, Lord of the Tournament, appeared as challenger in the next tilt. He was clad in a complete suit of richly gilded armour, which far outshone in brilliancy the panoply of his compeers. His noble mien and magnificent appearance, the beauty of his charger, and his skill in the management of the animal, drew down the repeated acclamations of the multitude. Nor was his opponent, the Knight of the Dragon, the Marquess of Waterford, observed with less interest by those who could identify him by his device. From the opposite ends of the barrier, the distinguished knights, attended each by an esquire, rushed on to the combat; the Knight of the Dragon, plunging his rowels into the sides of his horse, impetuously urging to its utmost speed the noble animal, over which he had complete mastery, while the Lord of the Tournament advanced in stately pride, but yet with scarcely less velocity, on his well managed charger, till they met in the middle of their career. The Lord of the Tournament shivered his lance on the shield of his opponent, which rang with the stroke, and the victor was saluted by the greetings of his esquires and the enthusiastic acclamations of the spectators, gratified with the skill displayed in the encounter. In the second course both knights missed, but, in the third, the noble Earl again broke his lance on the armour of his opponent. After another burst of applause the noble Earl, amidst continued shouts and martial music of the band, rode up to the gallery and paid his devoirs to the Queen.

" The next challenger was the Knight of the Burning Tower, who was opposed to the Red Rose. In the first course the former hit his adversary. In the second the lance of the Knight of the Burning Tower was shivered and thrown high in the air, and the top of the lance of the other combatant was also broken. In the third the Knight of the Burning Tower broke his lance on the helmet of the Knight of the Red Rose, and a burst of acclamation rent the air in honour of the knight who had so gallantly borne himself in the *rencontre*, which was not less skilfully conducted than that of the preceding combatants.

" When Sir F. Hopkins had paid his devoirs to the Queen of Beauty, the Knight of the Black Lion, and the Knight of the Gaël, proceeded to the extremities of the barrier. In the first course both knights missed; in the second, the Knight of the Black Lion struck the Knight of Gaël's lance; and in the third course, the Knight of the Black Lion broke his lance against the armour of his opponent."

In the fifth tilt, the Marquess of Waterford encountered Lord Alford. In the first passage both passed without hitting or being hit; but, in the second passage, Lord Alford struck the noble Marquess, and broke off the head of his lance. In the third passage, the lance of the Marquess of Waterford splintered upon the shield of his opponent, and the shouts of the spectators hailed him the victor. This concluded the tilting of the first day.

We subjoin, in order to render the account of this, the most important part of the Tournament, as correct and as ample as possible, the description of the Tilting, by another eye-witness of the various passages. It will be seen that there is some trifling discrepancy in the statements; that discrepancy is, however, trivial, and arose, no doubt, from the narrators being at different points of the ground, and from the great rapidity with which the encounters of the knights took place.

THE TILTING.

A challenge having been sounded, the first course took place between the Knight of the Swan, Hon. Mr. Jerningham, and the Knight of the Golden Lion, J. O. Fairlie, Esq. The parties, armed at all points, were conducted by the marshals to their positions, one at each end and on opposite sides of the barrier, where they remained till the heralds should announce the onset. The cry of " Laisser les Allez" being given, the heralds then sounded the charge, and the knights met at full gallop. For the sake of brevity we shall enumerate the courses as follows :—

1. Passed without striking.
2. Passed without striking.
3. False run. Hon. Mr. Jerningham's horse shying.
4. J. O. Fairlie, Esq.'s lance broken on opponent's shield. This closed the first tilt; after which the victor knight (J. O. Fairlie, Esq.), was conducted to the throne and made his obeisance to the Queen.

SECOND TILT.

Lord Eglinton, the Lord of the Tournament, and the Marquess of Waterford, Knight of the Dragon.
1. Both lances broken. (Great cheering).
2. The start being unequal, both passed without attempting to hit.

3. Lord Eglinton's lance splintered on the shield of the Marquess. (Renewed applause).

Lord Eglinton, the victor, was conducted to the throne by the marshal, as on the previous occasion. Both riders were well mounted, the Earl riding a gallant chesnut, and the Marquess a cream-coloured charger of high spirit and action.

THIRD TILT.

Sir F. Hopkins, the Knight of the Burning Tower, and R. J. Lechmere, Esq., the Knight of the Red Rose. This was a spirited bout.
1. Both struck. Sir F. Hopkins' lance broken on his opponent's shield. (Cheering.)
2. Both struck, and both lances broken. The lance of the Knight of the Burning Tower was broken foul on the helmet of the Knight of the Red Rose, whose lance was broken fairly on the shield of his adversary.
3. Sir F. Hopkins' lance again broken; his adversary having, from the severity of the previous shock, injured his hand, was unable to bring his lance to bear on his opponent. (Cheers.)—Sir F. Hopkins victor.

FOURTH TILT.

Lord Glenlyon, Knight of the Gael, and Lord Alford, Knight of the Black Lion.

1. Passed without hitting.
2. Crossed lances, but no damage sustained.
3. Lord Alford broke his lance on his opponent's shield, while the lance of Lord Glenlyon struck the helmet of Lord Alford, carrying away his feathers and other favours. During this encounter, it was curious to observe the interest manifested in the result by the retainers of Lord Glenlyon. Lord Alford the victor.

By way of varying the amusements, a combat now ensued, on foot, in front of the throne, between two swordsmen, Mr. M'Ian of the London Theatres, and an ensign of the Life Guards, each with a double-handed sword, and clothed in coats of mail. The performance was well enacted,—the parties laying about them with all the animation and prowess of an *outrance* encounter. The bout having been concluded, the heralds announced another challenge on the part of the knights, when the

FIFTH TILT

took place, betwixt the Marquess of Waterford and Lord Alford.
1. Passed without hitting.
2. Lord Alford struck his opponent, breaking the head off his lance.
3. Marquess of Waterford's lance splintered on the shield of his opponent. (Applause.)—Marquess victor.

Such were the knightly deeds in the lists on the first day (Wednesday) of the Tournament. On Friday, the tilting was renewed, and thus were the passages.

FIRST TILT.

Lord Glenlyon, the Knight of the Gael, and Viscount Alford, Knight of the Black Lion. The following was the order of the courses :—
1. Lances crossed—Lord Glenlyon's splintered.
2. Passed without hitting.
3. Do. do.
The tilt was not a very spirited one. The advantage lay with Lord Glenlyon, who was conducted by the marshal to pay obeisance to the Queen of Beauty.

SECOND TILT.

J. O. Fairlie, Esq., Knight of the Golden Lion, and the Earl of Craven, Knight of the Griffin.
1. The parties advanced rather cautiously, but both lances were shivered at the charge. (Great applause). Lord Craven's armour deranged by the shock.
2. Passed without hitting.
3. Lord Craven's lance having been splintered, he was declared the victor, and as such was led to the presence of the Queen, amid much applause.

THIRD TILT.

R. Lechmere, Esq., Knight of the Red Rose of

Lancaster, and the Earl of Eglinton, Lord of the Tournament.
1. Passed without hitting.
2. A pass of courtesy.
3. Lord Eglinton's lance broken, the crash reverberating through the lists (great applause), the shield of his opponent being broken by the shock. The Lord of the Tourney declared the victor.

Succeeding this tilt, the herald moved opposite the seat of the Queen of Beauty, and after repeating " O yes," three times, announced that an Unknown Knight had challenged the Knight of the Dolphin (Earl Cassillis). This created considerable excitement, for it was understood that the Unknown would be a German Prince of fame and fortune; but the challenger did not appear, and the challenge dropped.

FOURTH TILT.

W. L. Gilmour, Esq., the Black Knight, and the Marquess of Waterford, Knight of the Dragon.
1. Passed without hitting.
2. Do. do.
3. Do. do. Undecided.

FIFTH TILT,

between Lord Cassillis, Knight of the Dolphin, and Charles Lamb, Esq., Knight of the White Rose.

1. Passed without hitting.
2. Do. do.
3. Crossed lances, but neither had the advantage.

SIXTH TILT.

Hon. Mr. Jerningham, Knight of the Swan, and Captain Gage, Knight of the Ram.
1. Passed without hitting.
2. Unfair start,—a pass of courtesy.
3. Passed without hitting.

SEVENTH TILT.

J. O. Fairlie, Esq., Knight of the Golden Lion, and Sir Francis Hopkins, Knight of the Burning Tower.
1. Passed without hitting.
2. J. O. Fairlie, Esq., broke his lance on his opponent's shield.
3. Passed without hitting.—J. O. Fairlie, Esq., victor.

The Plate itself represents the third passage in the second tilt on the first day of the Tournament, at the moment when the lance of the Earl of Eglinton was shivered on the shield of the Marquess of Waterford.

The two esquires to the left of the spectator, are J. C. Mc Doual, Esq., and F. Cavendish, Esq. Sir C. Lamb is seen in the background galloping to the barrier, and holding up his warder, or staff of office. The Earl of Eglinton is nearly in the centre, and is the principal figure. On the other side of the barrier is his martial opponent, the Marquess of Waterford, and close behind him are his esquires, J. Ricardo, Esq., and Sir Charles Kent, Bart. The jester, Mr. Mc Ian, is on the extreme right. This was a most animating scene. The artist has caught the enthusiasm of the moment, and transmitted it through his pencil.

THE PLATE.

1. Sir Abr: Bradl: Esq: 2. F. Lascelles Esq: 3. Sir L: Scott Esq: 4. Marquess of Hastings 5. Sir Che: Wm: Bart 6. T. Earl of Salisbury 6. Max Zoller 7. Sir Che: Wm: Bart G. S. C. Rhodes Esq:

THE EGLINTON TOURNAMENT.

DESCRIPTION OF PLATE—No. XVIII.

The Mêlée.

"In doubtful battle, doubling blow on blow,
　Like lightning flamed their faulchions to and fro,
　And shot a dreadful gleam; so strong they strook,
　There seem'd less force required to fell an oak."
　　　　　　　　　　　　　　　　　DRYDEN.

"With him there wenten knights many on,
　Some wol armed in an habergeon,
　And in a breast plate, and in a gipon;
　And some wol have a pair of plates large,
　Some wol been armed on his legges wele,
　And have an axe, and some a mace of steel,
　There n' is no newe guise, that it n' as old:
　Armed they weren, as I have you told,
　Everich after his opinion."
　　　　　　　　　　　　　　　　　CHAUCER.

"When these Suns—
　For so they phrase them—by their heralds challeng'd

The noble spirits to arms, they did perform
Beyond thought's compass; that former fabulous story,
Being now seen possible enough, got credit."
　　　　　　　　　　　　　　　　　SHAKSPEARE.

"I wot yt 'was' ne chylder game; whan thay togedyr met,
　When icha freke in the feld on his feloy bet,
　And layd on styfly, for nothing wold thay let,
　And foght ferly fast, tyll their horses swet,
　　And few wordys spoken."
　　　　　　　　　　　　　　TOURNAMENT OF TOTTENHAM.

"The Eldridge knight was mickle of might,
　And stiffe in stower did stande,
　But Sir Cauline with a backward stroke,
　He smote on his right hand."
　　　　　　　　　　　　　　　　　SIR CAULINE.

THE tilting has been already described, and the Plate by which the description is illustrated is so accurate a representation of what actually took place at Eglinton, that even those who were not eye-witnesses of the Joust, can form a perfect idea from that alone, of this part of the warlike pastimes exhibited in the Lists, and in which the most exalted nobles and honourable men in the country were the performers. The same praise is due to this Plate, in which the artist has depicted, with the strictest fidelity to the facts, the sword combat of the "Mêlée."

The celebrated description of the "Passage of Arms" of Ashby-de-la-Zouch, which occurred in the reign of Richard the First, the "Lion-hearted" king, by Sir Walter Scott, has rendered all people of research and taste familiar with the modes of combat adopted by our ancestors; that description is, however, taken from the accounts of similar events with which the writings of Froissart abound. Those who would acquire a minuter knowledge of these mimic "feats of brawl and battle," will, in the chronicles of the last-named writer, an eye-witness of the scenes he paints, find ample employment for their leisure, and in the pages of the old romance writers may be found almost interminable narratives of Tilts and Tournaments, the Mêlée, and the Joust; and more particularly in the celebrated Spanish romance—"Amadis of Gaul"—will the taste of the lover of chivalry find gratification and amusement.

In this Plate, eight knights are seen engaged in the martial strife of the "Mêlée." The knights were—

The Earl of Eglinton	The Lord of the Tournament.	
The Marquis of Waterford	The Knight of the Dragon.	On the one side.
Walter Little Gilmour, Esq.	The Black Knight.	
Charles Lamb, Esq.	The Knight of the White Rose.	

R. J. Lechmere, Esq.	The Knight of the Rose of Lancaster.	
Viscount Alford	The Knight of the Black Lion.	On the other side.
The Honourable E. S. Jerningham .	The Knight of the Swan.	
J. O. Fairlie, Esq.	The Knight of the Golden Lion.	

The mêlée took place on that part of the Lists which extended between the "barrier" and the gallery in which the Queen of Beauty, her attendants, and the guests at the Castle were seated. There were in this gallery, besides many noble and distinguished persons whose names have already been mentioned, the following long list of the rank, fashion, and beauty of the three united kingdoms.

Ailsa, Marquess and Marchioness of
Annesley, Mr. and Mrs.
Agnew, Col. and Mrs.
Arthur, Dr. and Mrs.
Alexander, Mr. and Mrs., of Ballochmyle
Alexander, Mr. W. and B.
Aird, Mr., of Crossflat
Allison, Mr.
Auld, Mr.
Abercorn, Marquess of
Ashley, Lord and Lady
Alexander, Mrs., of Southbar

Baird, Sir D. and Lady Anne
Baird, Major and Miss
Blantyre, Lady, and Miss Stewart
Blair, Sir D. and Lady Hunter
Boswell, Mr. J. D., of Garallan, and the Misses
Blair, Colonel, and Mrs. Hunter, of Dunskey
Bell, Sheriff
Boyle, Lord Justice Clerk, and Mrs. and Misses, of Shewalton
Boyle, Mr. and Mrs. P.
Blair, Mr. W., younger, of Blair
Ballantyne, Mr., of Castlehill
Blair, Mr. B.
Blane, Mr.
Balfour, Mr.
Bedford, Mr. and Mrs.
Burnett, Mr. and Misses, of Gadgirth
Burgeish, Lord
Blane, Mr. and Mrs., of Seafield
Blackburn, Mr. and Mrs.
Back, Captain
Burges, John Yuge, Esq.
Buonaparte, Prince Louis
Belhaven, Lord and Lady
Boswell, Sir J., Bart.
Breadalbane, Marquess of
Brook, Mr.
Bogle, Mr., of Rosemount
Buchanan, Mr., younger, of Catrinebank
Burt, J. G. M.
Blackwood, Mr. A.

Crawford, Mr. and Miss, of Cartsburn
Crawford, T. M., younger, of Cartsburn, 93rd Highlanders
Cathcart, Sir John A.
Cathcart, Hon. Col. and Mrs. M.
Cunningham, Sir A., Crosshill
Cunningham Allison, Mrs., of Logan
Colville, Mr. and Mrs.
Clark, Col., and Misses Roger
Colbrook, Sir E.
Carnie, Dr.
Carter, Col., and officers of the 1st Royals
Campbell, Mr., of Sornbeg
Cunningham, Mr. and the Misses Smith, of Caprington
Cunningham, Misses
Campbell, Mr. and Misses
Campbell, Mr., Mrs., and Miss, of Craige
Campbell, Captain
Chambers, Mr. W., Edinburgh
Craecroft, Mr.
Crawford, Col., Mrs. and Misses, of Newfield
Carnie, Mrs. and Misses Turnbull
Clark, Mr.
Carnie, Mr. and Mrs.
Cunningham, F.
Charteris, Mr. F.
Crowen, Hon. F.
Cowan, Mr. and Miss
Crawfurd, Mr., Mrs., and Misses, of Craufurdland
Campbell, Mr. and Misses
Campbell, Mr. D.
Cochrane, Mr. and Misses
Cowan, Mr. and Misses
Carpendale, Mr., Mrs., and Miss
Charleville, Earl and Countess of
Cavendish, Hon. Frederick
Campbell, Mr. and Mrs. Garden, of Fifeshire
Cox, Captain
Corbould, Mr.
Crawford, Lieut.
Campbell, Sir H.
Chelsea, Lord
Carnwath, the Dowager Countess of
Cunningham, Mr., of Thornton

Crawford, Mr., of Doonside
Campbell, Mr. and Mrs., of Fairfield
Campbell, Mr. and Mrs., of Treesbanks
Craick, Mr. and Miss, of Arbigland
Colnaghi, Mr. Martin

Drumlanrig, Lord
Douglas, Marquess of
Douglas, Col., and Officers of the 78th Regiment
Des Devaux, Mr. and Lady Sophia
Dodd, Sir W.
Dunmore, Earl and Countess of
Dundas, Sir D.
Douglas, Lady J.
Dalrymple, Mr.
Davidson, Mr. and Mrs.
Donaldson, Dr.
Dunn, Captain and Mrs.
Davies, Rev. Mr.
Delachervies, Mr.
Dunlop, Mr. and Mrs.
Denham, Captain and Mrs.
Dalgleish, Mr.
Dow, Rev. Mr.
Denham, Captain, R. N., and Mrs. and Charles Denham, Esq.
Dowall, Mr.
Don, Sir William, Bart.
Dallas, Sir Robert and Miss
Darling, Mr. P.

Elliott, Sir W.

Finnie, Provost Kilmarnock
Fairlie, Miss, of Bellfield
Fullarton, Misses
Forbes, Mr., of Callendar
Forrester, Lord and Hon. Cecil
Fitzharris, Lord
Fairlie, Mrs., of Williamfield
Fairlie, Mr. and Mrs., of Holmes
Fergusson, Sir Charles and Lady
Fergusson, Mr., Mrs., and Miss
Fullerton, Mr., Mrs., and Miss
Farquharson, Col. and Mrs.
Fortesque, Mr.
Fortesque, Misses
Fullarton, Mrs. and Miss
Fergusson, Mr.
Fife, Earl of
Fairlie, Sir John and Lady Cunningham

Gordon, Sir John and Lady
Glenlyon, Lady and Misses Murray
Graham, Sir J. and Lady
Graham, Mr., of Netherby
Gordon, Sir R.
Gordon, Lieut.
Greenock, Lady and Miss Cathcart
Graham, Captain and Mrs.
Gilpin, Mr.
Gilmour, Mr.
Gray, Provost
Glasgow, Mr., Mrs., and Misses
Gascoigne, Mr. J.
Gascoigne, Mr.
Gisborne, Mr. and Mr. A.
Grieve, Mr.
Grant, Dr.
Gillies, Provost
Gordon, Mr. T., of Newton Lodge
Gray, Mr., of Glentig
Gray, Mr., younger, of Glentig

Hodgson, Mr.
Hill, Mr. D. O.
Hamilton, Col. and Mrs.
Himlockie, Sir J.
Hay, Sir Adam
Hunter, Mr. J.
Hunter, Mr. R.
Hamilton, Misses
Hunter, Mr. and Mrs., of Hunterston
Hope, Mr. and Mrs.
Holvett, Mr. C.
Hamilton, Miss
Hughes, Mrs.
Hopetoun, Lady, and Miss Macdonald
Houstoun, Miss
Hay, Messrs.
Hamilton, Mr. and Miss M.
Hamilton, Dr. and Mr. A.
Hamilton, Mrs. and Misses

Hay, Captain and Mrs., of Coilsfield
Hamilton, James, Esq.
Head, Sir Francis
Head, Sir George
Hamilton, A., Esq., of Carcluie, and Lady Jane
Hamilton, Mr. and the Misses, of Sundrum
Hamilton, Mrs. and the Misses, of Pinmore
Hunter, Mr., Mrs., and Miss, of Doonholm
Houston, Esq., M. P.
Hamilton, Colonel Hugh
Hunter, Mr. A.
Hamilton, Mr. and Mrs., of Braehead
Hunter, Mr. Campbell, 30th Regiment
Hodgson, Esq., M. P.

Irvine, Mr.
Ingestrie, Viscount

Jerningham, Hon. Mrs.
Johnstone, Mrs. and Miss
Johnstone, Mr.
Jamieson, Mr. and Mrs.

Kennedy, Col., Mrs. and Miss
Kearney, Lieut. Colonel and Mrs., and Officers of Queen's 2nd Dragoons
Kennedy, Captain
Kennedy, Rev. D.
Kennedy, Col., Mrs. and Miss
Kennedy, Mr. W.
Kent, Sir F.
King, Miss
Kelso, Colonel, of Dalkeith
Kelburne, Lord

Landseer, Mr.
Limond, Mr., R.
Limond, Provost, Mr. and Miss, of Dalblair
Lauder, Sir T. D.
Laurenson, Major
Leslie, Colonel and Lady
Logan, Misses
Lairdner, Mr.
Londonderry, Marchioness of
Luke, Mr.
Lestowell, Lady and Miss Burke
Lamb, Sir Charles, Lady Montgomerie, and Mr. Lamb
Lubeski, Count
Lizars, Professor

Macdonald, J.
Margesson, Mr., Mrs., and Miss
Montgomerie, Mr., of Belmont
Mackenzie, Mr.
Montgomerie, Major and Mrs., of Annick Lodge
Montgomerie, Captain and Miss
Macpherson, Major, Mrs. and Misses
M'Taggart, Captain
Mitchell, Mr., of Frankville
M'Aulay, Mr. and Miss
Miller, Mr. and Mrs.
Morris, Captain
M'Knight, Colonel
Maur, Lord Archibald St.
Martin, Major and Mrs.
Montgomery, Mr. W.
Montgomery, Captain
Maxwell, Captain and Mrs.
Montgomery, Mr. and Mrs.
Munroe, Sir Thomas
Macleod, Mrs. and Misses, of Macleod
Maitland, Mr. and Miss
Macallester, Colonel and Mrs.
Maidstone, Lord
M'Fadzean, Dr. and Mrs.
Montgomery, Mr.
Montgomery, Mr. C.
Montrose, Duke and Duchess of
Maxse, Mr. and Lady Caroline
Mexborough, Countess of
M'Dowall, Captain
Macdonald, Hon. J.
Macdoual, Hon. Mr. and Mrs. Grant
Miller, Mr., of Monkcastle

Neill, Col., Mrs., and Misses, of Swinridgemuir
Niven, Mr.
Norie, Mr. and Mrs.
Nisbett, Mr. T.
Nixon, Mr. J. H.

Ogilvie, Sir J. and Lady
Ovens, Mr.
Ossulton, Lord
Onslow, Mr. and Mrs. Arthur

Parker, Mr.
Pearce, Mr. and Mrs.
Paterson, Mr., Mrs., and Miss
Proven, Mr. J.
Patrick, Mr. and Mrs. T.
Pollock, Dr.
Persigny, Count
Powerscourt, Lord
Pettat, Captain
Purvis, Captain

Queensberry, Lord and Lady

Ritchie, Mr. and Mrs., of Cloncaird
Ralston, Mrs.
Ross, Mrs. and Miss
Ross, Captain
Robertson, Mr.
Ranken, Mr. and Mrs., of Drumley
Ritchie, Rev. Dr.
Reid, Captain
Ralston, Mr. and Mrs.
Robinson, Captain
Rendlesham, Lady and Misses Thelluson
Ricardo, Mr. L.
Raith, Colonel
Rollo, Hon. Roger, Mrs. and the Misses
Rishe, Captain and Miss
Reilly, Mr., Mrs., and the Misses
Reilly, Mr. John
Reilly, Mr. John Temple
Ramsay, Mr., of Barnton
Richardson, Rev. John

Stuart de Rothsay, Lord and Lady, and Miss Stuart
Speirs, Mr. and Mrs.
Stirling, Mr., Mrs., and Miss
Stewart, Mr.
Steven, Mr. and Mrs.
Shaw, Mr. and Mrs.
Smith, Mrs.
Sym, Miss
Stirling, Mr. and Mrs., of Gargunnoch
Suffolk, Lord and Lady Howard
Savage, Mr. and Mrs.
Sutherland, Mrs.
Stuart, Lady and Miss
Strangeways, Hon. Mr.
Stirling, Sir J., R. N., and Lady
Scott, Mr. and Mrs.
Seaham, Lord
Seymour, Lord and Lady
Stanley, Mr. and Mrs.
Standen, Colonel
Stevenson, Captain
Saville, Lady Sarah
Shortrede, Captain P.
Shortrede, Mr. A.
Scott, Mr. T. R.
Spackman, Mr. W. F.

Tennent, Mr.
Todd, Major
Tait, Captain
Thomson, Captain
Turnbey, Mr.
Tullamore, Lord

Upton, Mrs. and Miss

Villiers, Hon. F.
Vane, Lord Francis
Vivian, J. H., Esq.

Whiteside, Dr. W.
Whiteside, Dr. and Mrs.
Wallace, Sir M. and Lady
Wilson, Mr.
Wood, Colonel
Wood, Mr.
Wilson, Professor
Warner, Dr.
Walker, William, Esq.
Williamson, Mr.
Warren, Mr. Blair
Wombwell, Mr. and Mrs. Charles
White, Hon. Mr.

Zetland, Lord

The opponent knights were stationed at the extremeties of this arena:—four at one end, and four at the other. The Knight Marshal of the Lists, Sir Charles Montolieu Lamb, with his assistant-marshals, warders, and a strong escort of men-at-arms, on horseback, took his station on the right of the long gallery, in readiness to interpose his authority, if need should be for his interference, and to enforce the regulations of the combat. The knights and esquires not engaged in the *mêlée*, formed in groups upon the verge of the apportioned ground, and the high functionaries of the Tournament were all at the respective posts assigned them by the laws of chivalry and the rules of the day.

It was a stirring scene. The eyes of thousands were strained to witness the prowess of the combatants, who with difficulty restrained the ardour of their neighing steeds, and waited with impatience the signal of the heralds.

> " ———————— Si qua Sonum procul arma dedere,
> Stare loco nescit, micat auribus, et tremit artus,
> Collectumque premens volvit sub naribus ignem."

" He paweth in the valley, and rejoiceth in his strength: he goeth on to meet the armed men."

" He mocketh at fear, and is not affrighted; neither turneth he back from the sword."

" He swalloweth the ground with fierceness and rage: neither believeth he that it is the sound of the trumpet."

" He saith among the trumpets, Ha! ha! and he smelleth the battle afar off, the thunder of the captains and the shouting."

At length the trumpets gave the signal for the charge, and the warlike words—" *Laissez les Aller*" were heard. There was no delay, the knights advanced at a gallop, and met each other in "mid career." The rules of the Tournament restricted the number of blows to be given and received, and restrained the combatants from the full development of those warlike impulses which the excitement of the moment could not fail to create. It was well those rules were stringent, and enforced by the authority of such a knight-marshal of the Lists as Sir Charles Montolieu Lamb; but for his firmness of resolution, well-timed interposition, and almost ubiquity of presence, the heated blood of those engaged might have carried the imitation of war to its reality, or, at least, might have produced results to be regretted in their cooler moments, by those who met as friendly opponents. The eight knights met and exchanged blows with right good will. Unfortunately the gauntlet of the Knight of the Swan, either from being not properly secured, or from some defect in the rivets by which the scales were connected, proved insufficient to protect the wrist of the wearer from the ponderous sword wielded by the strong arm of the Black Knight to whom he was opposed. The gauntlet was cut through, and a wound inflicted, which might have proved of dangerous consequences but for the prompt attendance of Dr. Guthrie, of Ayr, who was fortunately a spectator of the combat, and who instantly tendered his chirurgical assistance; the wounded gentleman, who had also received a stunning blow on his casque, was conveyed from the Lists, and carried by his attendants to his pavilion, where the requisite means for his recovery were afforded by the learned leech just mentioned. The Honorable Mr. Jerningham suffered severely from the effect of this wound; but happily recovered after a temporary confinement.

Two of the combatants—the Knight of the Dragon, the Marquess of Waterford, and his valiant adversary, the Knight of the Black Lion, Lord Alford, reined up their foaming steeds, and, more intent upon signalizing their prowess and their skill in the use of their weapons, than strictly obedient to the laws of the combat—a pardonable offence and one scarcely to be avoided in the hey-day of youthful blood, and amidst the excitements of the moment—were about to commence a conflict that might have realized the scenes of the olden time, and carried out the incidents of the Tournament beyond what was intended or contemplated by the noble Earl of Eglinton. Happily the Knight Marshal of the Lists, whose eagle eye surveyed all parts of the field, was at hand. That gallant knight, putting spurs to his horse, thrust in between the knightly opponents, and with his staff of office, held up in token of command, restrained their somewhat too impetuous ardour. The knights were in a moment obedient to this great functionary; they obeyed the command, and, by so doing, illustrated how well they knew the duties imposed by chivalry, and how completely they were subservient to its laws. With this display of valorous achievement, the sports of the day concluded, and the cavalcade returned to the Castle. The scene was most splendid, the spectators were carried backward four hundred years; they beheld the realization of the ages of the conqueror, of the crusades, the fields of Agincourt and Cressy. The glowing descriptions of old chroniclers were acted before their eyes; they lived in the best days of glorious chivalry!

THE EGLINTON TOURNAMENT.

DESCRIPTION OF PLATE—No. XIX.

The Presentation of the Knight.

"Let wreaths of triumph now my temples twine,
The victor cried, the glorious prize is mine."
POPE.

"The people rend the skies with vast applause;
All own the chief, where fortune owns the cause."
CHAUCER.

"None was disgraced; for falling is no shame;
And cowardice alone is loss of fame.
The venturous knight is from the saddle thrown;
But 'tis the fault of fortune, not his own,
If crowds and palms the conquering side adorn."
IBID.

"In court whoso demandes,
What dame doth most excel;
For my conceit I must needes say,
Fair *Seymour* bears the bel.

"Upon whose lively cheeke,
To prove my judgment true,
The rose and lillie seeme to strive,
For equall change of hewe.

"And therewithall so well
Hir graces all agree;
No frowning cheere dare once presume,
In her sweet face to bee."
GASCOIGNE.

ERY triumphantly, and like a stalworth knight, did the gallant Earl of Eglinton carry himself in the joust and the *melée*, and loud were the acclamations of the spectators as he rode towards the throne of the Queen of Beauty to receive the wreath of victory, rendered doubly valuable from being presented by the fair hand of the sovereign lady of the sports. This was one of the most important scenes in the Tournament, a respite from the more warlike labours of the Lists, and an elegant episode in the passages of arms. The ceremony of the presentation of the victorious knight to the lady who presided over the martial games was arranged in strict accordance with the practices of the more early days of chivalry, nothing was omitted in this ceremonial, which was in usage in the days of the ancestors of the noble knights, esquires, dames, and damoiselles assembled, and nothing was introduced for which there was not the strictest warrant in the records of the middle ages. The Plate represents the facts and circumstances, the splendour and pomp of this part of the Tournament, with perfect accuracy. The Gothic gallery, in which the throne of the Queen of Beauty was erected, forms the back ground of the picture, it was filled by a collection of the rank and beauty of the empire, habited in costumes, by which the brilliancy of their charms was, if possible, increased and enhanced, or, rather, set forth more favourably than by the modern fashions of these days. The effect was splendid, delightful to the eye and ravishing to the senses.

"The looking on would make old Nestor young."

In the centre is seen the Lady Seymour, habited in the appropriate regal robes of her high estate, and crowned with the coronet of her office.

"Made to engage all hearts and charm all eyes."

Her ladyship holds the wreath which she is about to bestow upon the Lord of the Tournament. At this moment every eye was bent upon the fair monarch of the Lists, and every heart was captivated with her beauty, her grace, her mingled dignity, and affability of manner.

"Graced with all that charms the heart,
Blushing nature, smiling art."

The presentation is made by the Knight Marshal of the Lists, who raises his baton of office, and declares to the Queen of the Tournament the name of the successful champion.

In the gallery, besides the ladies attendants on the Queen of Beauty and the ladies visitors, &c., are seen Lord Bulkeley and also Prince Louis Napoleon Buonaparte, who was one of the illustrious guests at Eglinton Castle during the whole of the Tournament, and distinguished himself, not only by his affability, companionable qualities, and elegant demeanour, but by his repeated exhibitions of his proficiency in the use of the sword, and in his knowledge of the use of the weapons of the ages of chivalry. The subsequent history of this Prince is in the recollection of everybody, and whatever may be the political notions of those who have marked his public career, there can be but one opinion of his amiable and admirable qualities in private life amongst those who are familiar with his manners and pursuits, and who were honoured with his society whilst in this country. But now—

"The baffled prince in honour's flattering bloom
Of hasty greatness finds the fatal doom."

The esquires of the knight and a deputy marshal are on foot. The other persons represented are Lord Saltoun, Lord Glenlyon, the Marquess of Waterford, the Hon. Mr. Jerningham, and Captain Farlie.

The lower border of the frame represents archers, reclining Cupids, with bows, arrows, and quivers.

THE ABDICATION OF MARY QUEEN.

THE EGLINTON TOURNAMENT.

DESCRIPTION OF PLATE—No. XX.

The Banquet.

" A table richly spread in regal mode,
  With dishes piled, and meats of noblest sort
  And savour, beasts of chase, or fowl of game,
  In pastry built, or from the spit, or boil'd
  Gris-amber-steam'd ; all fish from sea or shore,
  Freshet, or purling brook, of shell or fin,
  And exquisitest name.
  And at a stately sideboard by the wine
  That fragrant smell diffused, in order stood
  Tall stripling youths rich clad, of fairer hue
  Than Ganymed or Hylas.
  Nymphs of Diana's train, and Naides,
  With fruits and flowers from Amalthea's horn,
  And ladies of the Hesperides, that seem'd
  Fairer than feign'd of old, or fabled since
  Of faery damsels met in forest wide
  By knights of Logres, or of Lyones,
  Lancelot, or Pelleas, or Pellenore ;
  And all the while harmonious airs were heard
  Of chiming strings, or charming pipes, and winds
  Of gentlest gale Arabian odours fann'd
  From their soft wings, and Flora's earliest smells."
                        MILTON.

" You shall have Rumney and Malmesyne,
  Both Ypocrasse and Vernage wyne :
  Mountrose, and wyne of Greke,
  Both Algrade and Respice eke,
  Antioche and Bastarde,
  Pyment also and Garnade :
  Wyne of Greke and Muscadell,
  Both Clare Pyment and Rochell,
  The reed your stomach to defye,
  And pottes of Osey set you by."
             SQUHR OF LOWE DEGRE.

" The banquet and the song—
  The revel loud and long :
  This feast outshone the banquets past."
                    SCOTT.

" ————— and the strong table groans
  Beneath the smoking sirloin, stretch'd immense
  From side to side, in which, with desperate knife,
  They deep incision make, and talk awhile
  Of England's glory, ne'er to be defaced,
  While hence they borrow vigour : or amain
  Into the pasty plunged."   THOMSON.

ORTHY of the universal praise bestowed upon it was the Banquet, than which nothing could have been imagined more splendid in appearance or more admirable in its arrangements : it was held in a large temporary erection close to the Castle, under the directions of the Messrs. Pratt. From the Castle to this apartment the passage was from the grand staircase, which, with the passage itself, was lit up in the most brilliant style, and decorated with rows of exotic plants, rare shrubs, and flowers. The effect was magical, and, as the guests entered, the whole, from the splendour of the costumes, the variety of the decorations, the mingled colours of the banners, the gorgeous richness of the plate, and the brightness diffused on every part by the innumerable tapers by which the whole was lit up, gave an idea of the revels of Faëry Land :

" Of some gay creatures of the element."

At the end of this noble hall the band of the Second Dragoon Guards was placed, dressed in the costume of the age in which such banquets were of more frequent occurrence, and playing some of the best adapted concerted music, under the direction of Mr. Wilman. The tables were laid for upwards of four hundred guests, all of whom were served upon massive silver during the repast, and upon gold during the dessert. The most exquisite dishes which the culinary skill of modern days could supply, together with the more antiquated, yet not less costly, viands of the days of chivalry, covered the tables. The pasty, the boar's head, the baron of beef, all were in aid of the lighter *entremets*. Wines of all kinds sparkled in the cups and glasses. The refinement of modern days was ingrafted on the sturdier wassail of the ancestry of those who partook of this noble banquet, and formed the grand, imposing, noble, and never-to-be-forgotten *reunion* of the lovely, the exalted, and the brave.

Amongst the guests were the following, who were located within the Castle during the sports of the Tournament :—

Marquess and Marchioness of Londonderry.	Lord Saltoun.	Sir Francis Head.	Lady Sarah Saville.
Lord Seaham.	Sir F. Hopkins, knight.	Sir George Head.	Lord and Lady Stuart de Rothsay.
Lady Francis Vane.	Marquess of Abercorn.	Lady Glenlyon.	Miss Stuart.
Lord and Lady Seymour.	Lord Cranstoun.	Misses Murray.	Mr. and Lady Jane Hamilton.
Hon. Cecil Forrester.	Lord Suffolk and Lady Howard.	Sir Hugh Campbell.	Lieutenant Crawford.
Lord Archibald Seymour.	Prince and Princess Esterhazy.	Sir M. Wallace.	Lieutenant Gordon.
Mr. Irvine.	Lord Archibald St. Maur.	Sir William Dunn.	Captain Stevenson.
Mr. and Mrs. Grant Macdoual.	Lord Zetland.	Captain Pettat.	Mr. and Mrs. Garden Campbell.
Lord and Lady Charleville.	Lord Powerscourt.	Mrs. and Miss Upton.	Lord Kelburne, M.P.
Lord Tullamore.	Lord Leven.	Mr., Mrs. and Miss Margesson.	Colonel Standen.
Mr. Purvis.	Hon. J. Macdonald.	Countess Dowager of Listowel.	Mr. Williamson.
Marquess of Waterford, knight.	Prince Louis Napoleon and Aide de Camp.	Miss Bushe.	Captain Cox.
J. O. Fairlie, Esq., knight.	Sir Charles Lamb.	Mr. White.	Lord and Lady Charleville.
W. L. Gilmour, Esq., knight.	Lady Montgomerie.	Lady Rendlesham.	Viscount Maidstone.
Earl of Cassillis, knight.	Mr. Lamb.	Miss Thellusons.	Viscount Alford.
R. Lechmere, Esq., knight.	Duke and Duchess of Montrose.	Lord and Lady Belhaven.	Viscount Myestre.
Lord Alford, knight.	Lord Chelsea.	Mr. and Miss Orby Wombwell.	Lady Caroline Maxse.
Lord Craven, knight.	Captain M'Dowall.	Countess of Mexborough.	J. H. Vivian, Esq., M.P.
Lord Glenlyon, knight.			

The Queen of Beauty sat on the right hand of the Lord of the Tournament, by whom she was handed to her chair, and on the left hand of the noble knight sat the Marquess of Londonderry, the King of the Tournament. The rest of the ladies were handed to their respective seats by the knights, and sat promiscuously, without any regard to rank, all being considered equal, and knighthood being the highest recognised grade on the occasion, a practice in strict keeping with the laws of chivalry.

The noble Lord of the Tournament, having proposed the health of the " Queen of Beauty," the toast was hailed with enthusiasm, amidst the cheers of nobles, knights, and esquires. The King of the Tournament, on behalf of the Queen of Beauty, acknowledged the compliment done to that fair and noble lady, and proposed the health of Lord Glenlyon, which having been received with the honours becoming the occasion, his lordship returned thanks. The health of the Lord of the Tournament was then proposed and received with acclamation, and drunk in a manner which evinced at the same time the zeal of the illustrious party for the honour of chivalry, their respect for the noble Earl, and the full and perfect sense they entertained for his exertions in the revival of the ancient Tourney, and the boundless hospitality displayed for the gratification of all who had the honour of being his guests. His lordship returned thanks. The ladies shortly afterwards retired, and the knights, having drank a few more toasts, left the banquetting hall to attend their partners in the ball-room.

The Plate represents this brilliant scene as accurately as the skill of the most accomplished artist can portray. It is, however, scarcely possible for the united labours of him who writes and of him who paints to convey to the reader and the spectator an adequate notion of its splendour. Those who were present will remember this scene with delight—

" Olim meminisse juvabit "

will be their motto and their happy privilege.

THE EGLINTON TOURNAMENT.

DESCRIPTION OF PLATE—No. XXI.

The Ball.

" Haste thee, nymph, and bring with thee
  Jest and youthful Jollity,
  Quips, and cranks, and wanton wiles,
  Nods, and becks, and wreathed smiles,
  Such as hang on Hebe's cheek,
  And love to live in dimple sleek ;
  Sport that wrinkle Care derides,
  And Laughter holding both his sides.
  Come, and trip it, as you go,
  On the light fantastic toe."
                                    L'ALLEGRO.

" Fair silver-buskin'd nymphs, as great and good ;
  I know this quest of yours, and free intent,
  Was all in honour and devotion meant
  To the great mistress of yon princely shrine,
  Whom with low reverence I adore as mine ;
  And, with all helpful service, will comply
  To further this night's glad solemnity."
                                    ARCADES.

" Methinks I hear, methinks I see,
  Sweet musicke, wondrous melodie,
  Rare beauties, gallant ladies shine,
  Whatever is lovely or divine ;
  All other joys to this are folly."
                                    BURTON.

" ——————— alone
  Know they to seize the captivated soul,
  In rapture warbled from love-breathing lips ;
  To teach the lute to languish ; with smooth step,

  Disclosing motion in its every charm,
  To swim along and swell the mazy dance."
                                    THOMSON.

" By day the Tourney, and by night
  The merry dance traced far and light ;
  The masquers quaint, the pageant bright,
  The dazzling lamps from gallery gay,
  Cast on the guests a dancing ray.
  Here to the harp did minstrels sing,
  There ladies touch'd a softer string :
  With long-ear'd cap, and motley vest,
  The licensed fool retailed his jest,
  While some in close recess apart
  Courted the ladies of their heart,
  Nor courted them in vain ;
  For often in the parting hour
  Victorious Love asserts his power.

" Light was his footstep in the dance,
    And firm his stirrup in the Lists,
  And, oh ! he had that merry glance
    That seldom lady's heart resists :
  Lightly from fair to fair he flew."
                                    SCOTT.

" For revels, dances, masks, and merry hours,
  Fore-run fair love, strewing his way with flowers."
                                    SHAKSPEARE.

YOUTH and beauty shone resplendent in the varied costumes of the company, and universal was the admiration expressed at the appearance of the ball-room. At one end of this superb apartment was placed a canopy, the draperies of which were disposed with great taste, fringed with silver ; it was surmounted with plumed coronets, as shown in the plate, and lined with cloth of gold, splendidly emblazoned with armorial bearings. Beneath the canopy were placed chairs of state, of the age of Louis XIV., and lower on the double *dais* were *fauteuils*. The principal seats were occupied by the Lord of the Tournament, the Queen of Beauty and the King of the Tournament, as described by the artist ; whilst, on the others, were seated many of the illustrious guests, and the pages of the great functionaries, officers, and ladies. The whole was illuminated by hundreds of tapers, suspended in brilliant chandeliers, and placed in antique candelabra. Large as was this noble room, it was almost crowded with dancers and spectators. The orchestra, which was under the superintendence of Mr. Wilman, of London, assisted by Mr. Thomson, of Glasgow, was admirably arranged ; it was placed at the side of the ball-room, and filled with musicians of first-rate reputation.

The dancing commenced at twelve o'clock, and was kept up with the spirit and animation which youth and beauty reciprocally inspire, the company retiring for a short interval into the banquet-room to partake of the refection necessary to support almost continuous exertion. It was five o'clock before the termination of the ball, and long had the sun shone forth upon this gay company before all was hushed in the repose which was to recruit them for fresh pleasures and fresh deeds of knightly pastime.

In the plate, an accurate representation of the appearance of the ball-room at one o'clock is given. On the extreme left, are portraits of Mr. Lamb and the Marchioness of Londonderry, who are in conversation. Beneath the canopy are portraits of the Earl of Eglinton, Lady Seymour, and the Marquess of Londonderry, and next to them is a portrait of Miss Montgomery. In the back ground are dancers thickly clustered in the evolutions of the dance ; and at the foot of the *dais*, in the foreground, a page is seated. Next to the page there is a group of four ; they are portraits of Lord Craven, the Marquess of Waterford, the Duke of Montrose, and the Marquess of Douglas ; the first three are habited in velvet and ermine ;

the fourth wears a tunic with belt and dagger. Lady Saville and Prince Louis Napoleon come next, as waltzers; then Mr. Ricardo, and Mr. Gilmour, who are also waltzing; and Mr. and Mrs. Garden Campbell in conversation.

The frame of this beautiful plate represents musicians in ancient costumes, and Cupids supporting coronets, and wreathed with roses.

An account in detail of the superb costumes in which the principal personages, both male and female, present at this matchless festival of chivalry were habited at the ball is subjoined; it will convey some notion of a scene which will live long in the annals of all that is great, noble, imposing, and magnificent.

THE COSTUMES.

The Dames and Damoiselles.

LADY SEYMOUR—THE QUEEN OF BEAUTY.

Morning.—Saya of violet velvet, having armorial bearings in front, emblazoned in silver on azure velvet; jacquet of meniver, spotted with ermine; partelet of sky-blue satin, worked with silver; mantle of rich crimson velvet, furred with meniver; gauntlets embroidered and fretted with gold; crown of silver, set with rich jewels.

Evening.—A superb antique brocade silk kirtle, raised with silver, gold, and various colours; vest of white velvet, with demi-sleeves of silver tissue damask wire; placard of gold, set with precious stones; skayne (or veil) of silver canvass, and chaplet of flowers.

DUCHESS OF MONTROSE.

Morning Costume.—Dress of ruby velvet, having armorial bearings on left side, emblazoned in gold on corn-flower blue velvet; jacket, black velvet, trimmed with meniver, with hanging sleeves faced with meniver; long tight velvet sleeves; upper part of bodice ornamented with jewels; mantle of corn-flower blue velvet trimmed with meniver. Head-dress, a cap of blue velvet barred with gold, over which was worn a coronet of stones set in gold. Gauntlets embroidered with gold.

Evening Costume.—Petticoat of rich cerise velvet, relieved by a breadth of silver-watered cloth, richly ornamented with precious stones; jacket of silver cloth trimmed with Russian sable; hanging sleeves, lined with cerise, and turned up with sable facings; long tight sleeves of silver, fastened at the wrist with emeralds and diamonds. Head-dress, a magnificent tiara of diamonds, with pendent veil of silver canvass. Gauntlets embroidered with silver.

THE MARCHIONESS OF LONDONDERRY.

A jacket of ermine, the skirt of violet velvet, with the front of sky-blue velvet, on which are her ladyship's arms richly embroidered in silver, and a coronet ornamented with jewels. This gorgeous apparel was prepared at Holdernesse House, under the noble lady's personal direction.

LADY MONTGOMERIE.

A riding costume of the 15th century, composed of a dress of royal blue velvet, with hanging sleeves lined throughout with rich white satin, and trimmed with mat gold; tight sleeves, body and under-robe in gold damas. Head-dress of royal blue velvet, ornamented with precious stones, and pendent veil embroidered in gold. Mantle of red and blue velvet, with arms embroided:—Quarterly, first and fourth azure, three fleurs-de-lis or; second and third gules, three amulets, or, each adorned with a gem azure; the whole within a bordure, or, charged with a tressure flory, counter flory, gules.

An evening costume of the same epoque, composed of rich white satin, brocaded in gold and coloured flowers; body elegantly trimmed with a gold guipure; berthe with long ends, long hanging sleeves, looped up with cord and tassels in real gold, and tight under-sleeves. Head-dress of sky-blue velvet, with a quarille of precious stones, edged with gold fringe, with a rich Brussels veil, falling gracefully over the shoulders.

Another evening costume of rich cerise and white damas, dress trimmed round with old point lace, headed by a buoffant, open in front, with an under-dress of white satin, embroidered in cherry-colour. Head-dress of guipure lace, tastefully adorned with cameos.

COUNTESS OF HOPETOUN.

Morning costume of the 15th century, composed of a dress of rich black velvet, embroidered in gold, with kirtle edged round with gold fringe; chemisette of goffered Indian muslin.

COUNTESS OF CHARLEVILLE.

Morning Costume.—Dress of crimson velvet, with armorial bearings on left side emblazoned in gold on blue velvet; jacket of emerald green velvet, trimmed with meniver, with hanging sleeves faced with meniver; long tight velvet sleeves; upper part of bodice ornamented with precious stones; mantle of emerald green velvet, trimmed with meniver. Head-dress, a cap of green velvet barred with gold, and coronet of precious stones set in gold. Gauntlets embroidered with gold.

Evening Costume.—Petticoat of rich silver brocade, relieved by breadth of sky-blue satin, edged with cerise, and festooned with bouquets of precious stones: jacket of ponceau velvet, trimmed with meniver blue bodice, and stomacher of jewels; hanging sleeves faced with meniver, and long tight blue satin sleeves embroidered with silver. Head-dress, a tiara of precious stones, with pendent veil of silver canvass. Gauntlets embroidered with silver.

Another evening costume in the reign of Henry VIII., composed of a mauve velvet surcoat, trimmed with gold lama, confined round the waist; with scarf of green and gold; under-dress of avanturine and white satin, trimmed with gold chef. Head-dress, a cap of green velvet ornamented with jewels.

THE COUNTESS OF MEXBOROUGH

Wore an Eastern costume, which attracted much attention.

COUNTESS OF DUNMORE.

A rich costume of the early part of the 15th century, consisting of a full robe of black velvet, trimmed with ermine, and ornamented with gold, over a petticoat of white satin, flowered and embroidered with gold. Head-dress, a caul of crimson velvet, trimmed with gold tissue.

LADY BLANTYRE.

A black velvet dress (costume, Anne Boleyn) trimmed with pearls and cordeliere of the same; under-dress of white satin, bordered with swan's-down, point lace tucker and ruffles. Head-dress of black velvet, and pearls in unison with the costume.

LADY LISTOWEL.

Morning.—A splendid black velvet dress and train, embroidered with gold; a rich gold-embroidered petticoat.

Evening.—Vest of black velvet, with a rich border of diamonds; silver bodice, and stomacher of diamonds; kirtle of antique Venetian silk, brocaded with gold and silver; tiara of diamonds.

LADY SARAH SAVILLE.

Morning.—Rich crimson velvet jaquet, furred with ermine, with gold bodice and stomacher of jewels; kirtle of green velvet; partelet of white lawn, embroidered with gold; coif of crimson velvet, studded with pearls.

Evening.—Pink satin "waistcoat," embroidered with silver, with falling sleeves, lined with silver tissue; kirtle of white satin, curiously wrought with silver; corse worked with gold and ornamented with jewels; veil of silver net.

LADY JANE HAMILTON.

A splendid dahlia satin dress, with superb ermine flounce, ornamented with rich gold; bodice, cord, and tassel to correspond. Head-dress of black velvet and rich gold; an Indian muslin veil, richly embroidered with gold.

LADY FRANCES VANE.

Morning Costume.—A robe, half of light blue and the other of silver cloth of gold; jacket, half of dark blue velvet, and the other of gold cloth de Russe, trimmed with swan's-down. A black velvet hat, trimmed with turquoise and brilliants.

LADY GRAHAM (of Netherby).

Morning Dress (of the time of Henry VII.)—A vest of blue velvet, confined round the throat by a splendid gorget of jewels; jacket of crimson velvet, trimmed with sable, the hanging sleeves caught up by a badge of jewels, and showing the under-sleeves of blue velvet wrought with gold; the front of the jacket was united by a bar of gold, closely studded with diamonds and mixed jewels; this was worn over a party-coloured velvet skirt, the front being blue, on which was richly embroidered in gold the family crest, "the eagle's wings." Her ladyship's mantle was of crimson velvet, lined with white satin, and trimmed with sable, and united across the chest by a bar of mixed jewels. Head-dress, violet velvet cap of the date of Henry VII., trimmed with gold, and confined round the head by a beautiful circlet of diamonds.

Second Morning Dress.—The marriage dress of Anne Boleyn, in materials and jewellery as splendid as the former dress; but the splendour and beauty of the cap worn with it had the greatest effect.

Evening Dress.—Robe of green velvet trimmed with ermine and jewels; the front of the corsage and round the bosom splendidly ornamented with jewels, and hanging sleeves, decorated to correspond, showed the under-sleeves, of white satin, embroidered with gold; the petticoat of rich antique gold brocade, with splendid border. The effect of this dress was greatly beautified by the large chain of pearls and jewels which reached from the waist to the border of the petticoat. Head-dress, cap, ornamented richly with diamonds and pearls, and a beautiful gold veil, with antique border.

Second Evening Dress.—Rich white velvet jacket, trimmed with meniver; hanging sleeves to match, lined with cherry-coloured satin, confined by clasps of jewels, and showing the under-sleeves of rich white and silver brocade; the bosom and front of the jacket covered with jewellery; skirt of white and silver brocade, worn over cherry-coloured satin, open at the side to show the cherry colour, and confined at intervals by large clasps of jewels. Head-dress, veil of silver net, edged with silver fringe, worn with a circlet of diamonds.

HON. MISS MACDONALD.

Morning Costume.—A neat kirtle of black velvet, with a jacket of the same material, trimmed with white fur. Head-dress of black velvet and pearls.

Evening Costume.—A plain costume du bal of rich white satin.

HON. MISS STUART.

Dress in the costume of Louis XVI., composed of rich cerise brocades; under-dress of white satin, flounced with lace; sleeves of white satin intermixed with cerise riband. Head-dress, a bouquet of mixed flowers on the left side.

HON. MISS FANNY STEWART.

The same.

MRS. CAMPBELL.

A morning dress of crimson velvet a queue; body, sleeves, and skirt ornamented with gold bouquets. Head-dress of gold lace and black velvet. Another morning dress of brocaded damas, the under-dress in white satin; body and sleeves trimmed with guipure lace; toque of Indian muslin, embroidered in silver. Evening dress of white satin; trimmed body, sleeves, and skirt, with dark blue velvet, and silver chef chaplet of bluets.

MRS. GARDEN CAMPBELL.

Evening Costume.—Ponceau velvet jacket trimmed with bullion fringe, gold bodice, and stomacher of jewels; hanging sleeves of velvet, with long tight sleeves of gold brocade; petticoat of rich silk brocade in colours, with gold brocaded breadth, trimmed with bullion fringe. Head-dress of ponceau velvet, trimmed with bullion fringe, and pendent veil of gold canvass.

MRS. CLAUDE ALEXANDER.

A morning costume of rich grenat velvet, body and sleeves trimmed with gold lace and fringe; the under-dress in rich satin, brocaded in with a black velvet toque, ornamented with pearls. Another morning dress of rich violet satin; tablier in white satin; body, sleeves, and skirt, trimmed with swan's-down; lace ruffles; scarf embroidered in gold. An evening costume of rich satin, brocaded *á la Pompadour;* body and sleeves trimmed with point lace, resille in pearls.

MRS. HUNTER BLAIR.

A rich dress of the fifteenth century, after the model of Margaret of Anjou.

MRS. MARGESSON.

A morning costume dress à queue of rich rose divine velvet, hanging sleeves, lined with white satin; body, sleeves, and skirt, richly hemmed with old point lace, under-dress of white satin, embroidered in gold, with tight sleeves ornamented with gold buttons; chemisette of goffered Indian muslin. Evening costume of same reign—a rich groseille velvet dress, tablier in white satin, embroidered in pearls; body, sleeves, and skirt, trimmed with old point lace and pearls; cordelier and ornaments to suit. Head-dress of old point lace, elegantly decorated with gold fringe.

MISS UPTON.

As "Beatrice of Ferrara," one of the maids of honour to the Queen of Beauty, wore a robe of pink gros de Naples of the richest description, having full trimmings of the same material, with ample sleeves, half long, turned back with rich point lace ruffles in the fashion of the day, with ancient jewelled armlets and bracelets. The whole style of the dress in the costume of Henri Quatre. It set off the wearer to great advantage. A ball-dress in costume of very rich white satin, with a silver and crepe lisse trimming, with silver tags. The berthe and ruffles of rich point lace, the stomacher covered with silver. The head-dress, a golden fillet with jewels; also a ball-dress in the costume of St. Louis; a jacket of pale blue velvet, lined throughout with white satin, closely fitting at the waist, embroidered with a deep border in silver; blue velvet open sleeves, embroidered in silver, with under-sleeves of white satin, having deep double ruffles of ancient point lace; an under-dress of rich white satin, with a Gothic trimming. The head-dress, a very small blue velvet cap, embroidered in silver, attached to the head with a silver arrow. A beautiful ball-dress of crepe lisse, over white satin, full trimmed with silver lace; over this a tunic of crepe lisse, over white satin, richly trimmed with silver. The head-dress, a turban embroidered in gold and imitation stones. This classical dress was in the Greek costume.

MISS MALCOLM.

A morning costume of sky-blue satin; dress tablier in white satin, trimmed round with swan's-down; hanging sleeves lined with white satin, and trimmed with swan's-down; black velvet toque, tastefully ornamented with pearls. Evening dress of white satin, trimmed with cerise velvet and gold. Head-dress of cerise velvet with white aigrette, and gold bows and fringe ends.

Evening Costume.—Jacket of scarlet and gold brocade, trimmed with bullion fringe, hanging sleeves of green and gold, Indian barbes; long tight sleeves of white satin; sto-macher of ditto, covered with enamels; petticoat of white satin, trimmed with green and gold barbes, edged with cerise velvet. Head-dress of cerise velvet, with white aigrette and gold bows and fringe ends.

MISS OCTAVIA MACDONALD.

A riding costume of the fifteenth century, composed of a dress of rich black velvet, lined throughout, and hanging sleeves; a kirtle of the same, trimmed round with ermine. Tasteful head-dress of black velvet, and pearls, in unison with the rest of the costume. An evening dress, composed of rich white satin; body, sleeves, and skirt trimmed with black velvet, and ornamented with pearls. Head-dress, a wreath of roses.

MISS BUSHE.

Evening.—Green velvet jacquet, richly ornamented with gold; bodice of gold set with jewels; gown of rich green and silver brocade, with kirtle of white gold and satin; chaplet of roses, and gold veil.

MISS MARGESSON.

A riding costume of the fifteenth century, composed of rich emerald velvet, with hanging sleeves, lined with white satin, edged round with gold, tight under-sleeves of white satin, fastened with gold buttons. Head-dress of white velvet, embroidered in gold, with long veil embroidered in gold. Evening dress of rich white satin, brocaded in gold en tablier, trimmed with several rows of wide gold fringe; hanging sleeves, trimmed with gold fringe; body, sleeves, and skirt, trimmed with bouffant in India muslin embroidered in gold. Head-dress of cerise velvet, ornamented with gold fringe, and coronet of precious stones set in gold.

THE MISSES CUNYNGHAME.

A rich, antique jacket, brocaded black and gold, trimmed with ermine; long tight sleeves of the same, the seduisantes of cerise silk, trimmed with ermine. Shirt of muslin, fitting close to the throat. Skirt of cerise-coloured silk. A superb mantle of pale apple-green, trimmed with broad gold, fastened in front by gold cord and tassel, but falling open. Head-dress, a pointed cap of antique fashion, composed of cerise and green satin, turned up with ermine. Evening head-dress, a coronet of gold, spiked with magnificent pearls.

Among the many most gorgeous dresses each lady exhibited daily at the Tournament, these were noticed as particularly graceful; though many others, elsewhere mentioned; many omitted, not less merit to be recorded. Among other very rich and beautiful dresses, which, as peculiarly adapted to the occasion, excited admiration, was a very rich dress of pale blue satin, having a deep border of ancient point lace round the petticoat, trimmed with knots of blue riband, with a close-fitting bodice and stomacher with point lace; slashed open sleeves, with very full under-sleeves of crepe lisse, in the costume of Rubens. A black velvet hat, with large Roman pearls, point lace, and plume of white ostrich feathers in the same costume.

A black velvet dress à la Marie Stuart, full trimmed with large Roman pearls, and an ancient cordeliere of the same, having an under-dress of white satin, also full trimmed with a Gothic bordering; the bodice close fitting, with a full point lace ruff; the double sleeves of black velvet lined with white satin, and trimmed with large Roman pearls and point lace ruffles. Head-dress corresponding.

The coiffures suitable to other beautiful dresses were gorgeous turbans, composed of gold point lace of the most curious and exquisite description.

Knights, Esquires, and Visitors.

THE MARQUESS OF LONDONDERRY,

THE KING OF THE TOURNAMENT.

Richly equipped in a cassock of emerald velvet, beautifully braided with gold, and trimmed with ermine. A brilliant collection of stars was displayed on his left breast, and the collar of the Order of the Bath was also worn by his Lord-ship. A diadem, surrounded by a cap-like covering of crimson velvet, with a large cluster of diamonds in the centre. Boots of crimson velvet, coming up to within a short distance from the knee, trimmed at the top with a gold gymp lace.

The Marquess wore the same splendid costume in the evening, with the exception of the full velvet mantle.

LORD SALTOUN,

THE JUDGE OF PEACE,

Robed in a cassock of rich black velvet, beneath which was a crimson satin shirt, confined at the waist by a crimson sword-belt, braided with gold; a mantle of puce velvet, trimmed with sable, covered the shoulders and back; a puce velvet cap, with a white ostrich feather, fastened by three costly jewelled clasps.

Evening.—A rich violet velvet tunic, bound with sable; a cloak of black velvet, bordered with sable; hose of violet silk, and russet boots, reaching near to the knee.

SIR CHARLES LAMB, BART.

THE KNIGHT-MARSHAL OF THE LISTS.

A demi-suit of black armour, exquisitely embossed with gold and silver, covered by a surcoat, on which were the arms of the Lambs and Montgomeries richly emblazoned.

Evening Costume.—A sky-blue silk velvet doublet, with full trunks, the doublet and sleeves slashed with white satin, and the bands braided with gold; a belt of crimson velvet, and scabbard covered with the same material, richly braided with gold; tight flesh silk hose, with blue kid ankle-boots, ornamented with gold braid.

THE EARL OF EGLINTON,

THE LORD OF THE TOURNAMENT.

A rich knight's costume of the fifteenth century; a short tunic of dark blue velvet, embroidered round the bottom with a motto, " Gardez-bien," fleur-de-lis, and an amulet, in gold; the sleeves of rich cloth of gold; white silk hose; ankle-boots of blue and yellow kid, braided with gold.

EARL OF CASILLIS.

A knight's costume of the time of Elizabeth, of crimson velvet trimmed and puffed with black, and richly embroidered with silver.

LORD GLENLYON.

An Elizabethan costume, made of rich tartan velvet (Athole and Murray), embroidered with gold; cap of the same; white silk hose.

VISCOUNT ALFORD.

Evening Costume.—A French blue silk velvet cassock, with long pointed sleeves, reaching below the knees, exquisitely braided and laced with silver; a dark blue satin shirt, confined at the neck by a silver band; cap of blue velvet, with a blue and white feather, clasped with a small aigrette of diamonds; ankle-boots, extravagantly pointed at the toes, embroidered with silver thread.

HON. CAPTAIN GAGE.

Evening Costume.—A costume de cour of the time of Eliza-beth, of a costly white cloth, superbly trimmed with a narrow gold lace, covered by a mantle or small cloak of blue silk velvet, lined with silk and braided with gold; an antique gold chain hung round the neck; cap of blue velvet, with a party-coloured feather of white and red.

HON. MR. JERNINGHAM.

Costume, embroidered with fleur-de-lis, and the Hadding-ton knot of crimson velvet, trimmed with gold; silver em-broidered sleeves; and white hose of the sixteenth century.

J. O. FAIRLIE, ESQ.

Evening Costume (date fifteenth century).—A magnificent cassock of crimson and blue velvet, with vest and full trunks of same, richly braided with gold; a loose cloak with large sleeves, embroidered with gold; cap of crimson velvet.

R. LECHMERE, ESQ.

Evening Costume.—A rich scarlet velvet tunic, with pointed sleeves, reaching within a short distance of the knee, braided with gold trimming; cap of scarlet velvet, with a red and white feather; a massive gold chain was suspended round the neck; ankle-boots of red leather, braided with gold.

CHARLES LAMB, ESQ.

Knight's costume of the fifteenth century; a black velvet tunic, embroidered with white roses, the sleeves of scarlet and gold embroidery; a crimson velvet belt, embroidered with the white rose, and motto, " Une Seule," in gold; lilac silk hose.

PRINCE NAPOLEON-LOUIS BUONAPARTE.

Morning Costume.—A highly polished steel cuirass, over a leather jacket, trimmed with crimson satin; a steel-vizored helmet, with a high plume of white feathers; white silk hose, and russet boots.

Evening Costume.—A short cassock of dark green velvet, with shirt and sleeves of crimson satin; a sword-belt or girdle of gold confined the waist; cap of crimson velvet, with a yellow feather fastened by a jewelled aigrette, falling gracefully over the left side; flesh-silk hose, with high boots, turned over red, and bound with gold lace.

DUKE OF MONTROSE.

Evening Costume.—A rich costume of the fifteenth cen-tury, of crimson velvet, sleeves lined with white satin, and trimmed with gold fringe; mantle of violet silk velvet, bordered with sable fur.

MARQUESS OF ABERCORN.

Morning Costume.—A beautiful Highland dress; jacket of green velvet, mounted with chased silver buttons; tartan and philibeg of the Hamilton plaid, with " a gude claymore down by his side."

Evening.—A costume of the time of Henry VIII., of scarlet velvet, embroidered with gold; a cloak of the same colour, lined with white satin; white silk hose, and scarlet ankle-boots, braided with gold.

MARQUESS OF DOUGLAS.

Morning Costume.—A splendid Highland costume, richly mounted; tartan, the Royal Stuart.

Evening.—Magnificent Venetian costume of black velvet.

EARL CRAVEN.

A knight's costume; the vest of rich scarlet velvet, puffed with white satin, and trimmed and embroidered with silver; trunks of the same; a cloak of scarlet satin, richly embroidered with gold, and trimmed with ermine; white silk hose.

COUNT VALENTINE ESTERHAZY.

An Elizabethan costume of scarlet velvet, embroidered with gold; white silk hose; scarlet cap and plume.

VISCOUNT FITZHARRIS.

Morning.—A plain Highland costume of mixed plaid.

Evening Costume.—A green velvet tunic with a broad collar, turned over with white satin, and trimmed with fur; flesh-coloured silk hose, with high shoes, beautifully braided.

VISCOUNT CHELSEA,

ESQUIRE TO THE KNIGHT-MARSHAL.

Morning Costume.—A cassock of white kerseymere, trimmed with blue velvet; cap the same, with a white feather.

Evening.—A tunic of emerald silk velvet, date the fifteenth century, coming up close to the neck; across his shoulders hung negligently a gold chain of great value, the whole of the dress being bordered with a bullion lace; cap of green velvet braided with gold, and a crimson feather placed care-lessly on the left side.

VISCOUNT OSSULSTON.

Evening Costume.—A costume of an early date, of scarlet velvet, bordered with ermine round the bottom and arm-holes; sleeves and vest of gold tissue; white silk hose, with white kid ankle-boots, braided with gold.

VISCOUNT MAIDSTONE.

Morning and Evening Costume.—A light green fine cloth vest and tunic, trimmed with gold lace, over which was a cuirass of black armour, with gorget elaborately embossed with gold and silver; shirt and sleeves of crimson satin, con-fined at the neck and wrists by small bands of gold lace; high boots, turned over with white squares; helmet of same embossed armour, with a full green and red feather. In the evening costume the cuirass and helmet were displaced, and instead of high boots the noble Viscount wore ankle-boots.

VISCOUNT PERSIGNY.

Evening Costume.—A dark blue cassock, open in front, and faced with white satin, with tight sleeves of a gold-figured material; cap of blue velvet, trimmed with gold braid; hose of flesh-coloured silk, with shoes of blue velvet, braided with gold.

LORD SEYMOUR.

Morning and Evening Costume.—A short doublet of hair-brown velvet, of the time of James I., confined at the waist by a broad black belt; the front crossed by stripes of blue gros de Naples; across the shoulders a scarf of sky-blue satin, tied in a knot on the left hip; high black boots, turned over with blue leather; cap of brown velvet and blue feathers.

LORD SEAHAM.

Morning Costume.—A rich dress of white satin, trimmed with small bands of crimson velvet and gold, covered by a mantle of scarlet velvet, trimmed with silver lace, and lined with white sarsenet; hose of crimson silk, boots of blue kid, richly embroidered with gold and coloured silk; cap of black velvet, with a white feather.

LORD JOHN BERESFORD.

Evening Costume.—Tunic of black silk velvet, collar turned over with white satin; sleeves and vest of silver tissue, with the crest of the Marquess of Waterford embroidered in coloured silks.

LORD KELBURNE.

An archer's costume of the fifteenth century.

LORD DRUMLANRIG.

An esquire's costume of the time of Elizabeth, of white cachemere, trimmed with gold, slashed and puffed with yellow satin; yellow satin cap and white plume.

SIR DAVID DUNDAS, BART.
ESQUIRE TO KNIGHT OF GAEL.

A costume of the fifteenth century; dark green velvet tunic, with sleeves of crimson and gold embroidery; vest of the same; crimson velvet cap and plume of dark blue feathers; white silk hose and purple velvet boots, with long pointed toes.

J. BALFOUR, ESQ.
ESQUIRE TO THE KNIGHT OF GAEL.

The same.

SIR R. DALLAS, BART.

An archer's costume of the fifteenth century.

SIR HUGH CAMPBELL, BART.

Evening Costume.—A green velvet cassock, with long pointed sleeves, lined with white sarsenet, richly trimmed with gold; a pouch of crimson velvet hanging from his sword-belt, ornamented with gold braid: cap of green velvet, with a white ostrich feather, fastened on the left side by a jewelled clasp.

THE HON. F. CHARTERIS,
ESQUIRE TO THE QUEEN OF BEAUTY,

Was attired in a rich puce silk velvet surcoat, open at the hips, elegantly embroidered with gold, and puffed at the shoulder and elbow with white satin, confined by narrow bands of gold lace; vest or shirt of splendid figured velvet; a small cloak of black velvet, braided profusely with gold; a broad sword-belt of crimson velvet; black boots, turned over with puce, and fringed with gold; hose of black silk.

F. CAVENDISH, ESQ.
ESQUIRE TO THE LORD OF THE TOURNAMENT.

A costume of blue velvet, slashed with gold-coloured satin, and embroidered with gold.

MR. G. DUNDAS,
ESQUIRE TO THE LORD OF THE TOURNAMENT.

The same.

GRANT M'DOUAL, ESQ.
ESQUIRE TO THE LORD OF THE TOURNAMENT.

The same.

SIR CHARLES KENT, BART.
ESQUIRE TO KNIGHT OF THE DRAGON.

A black velvet tunic, with broad white satin collar, the sleeves slashed and puffed with white, and trimmed with deep silver lace; an under-vest of silver; black velvet hat, trimmed with silver; plume of white feathers; and black and white striped hose.

HON. JAMES MACDONALD,
ESQUIRE TO THE KNIGHT OF THE GRIFFIN.

A scarlet tunic, trimmed with ermine; sleeves slashed with white satin, and ornamented with gold gymp lace; tight silk pantaloons, with low boots braided with gold.

HON. FREDERICK CRAVEN,
ESQUIRE TO THE KNIGHT OF THE GRIFFIN.

The same.

GARDEN CAMPBELL, ESQ.
ESQUIRE TO THE KNIGHT OF THE SWAN.

Evening Costume.—A crimson velvet doublet, embroidered with silver, from which issued sleeves of a costly material, of silver and various coloured silks, wrought into floral figures; cap of crimson velvet, slashed with white satin.

CAPTAIN STEPHENSON,
ESQUIRE TO THE KNIGHT OF THE SWAN.

The same.

MESSRS. COX AND WILSON,
ESQUIRES TO THE KNIGHT OF THE GOLDEN LION.

An esquire's costume of the fifteenth century, consisting of a tunic of dark blue velvet, embroidered with gold; crimson velvet sleeves, with bands of lace; crimson velvet cap and blue plume; crimson hose.

CAPTAIN PETTAT,
ESQUIRE TO THE KNIGHT OF THE GOLDEN LION.

The same.

CAPTAIN PURVES,
ESQUIRE TO THE KNIGHT OF THE GOLDEN LION.

The same.

CAPTAIN BLAIR,
ESQUIRE TO THE BLACK KNIGHT.

A costume of the time of Henry VIII., of black velvet, slashed and puffed with black satin; black silk hose; black velvet hat and plume.

C. CORRY, ESQ.
ESQUIRE TO THE KNIGHT OF THE RED ROSE.

A scarlet velvet tunic, embroidered with gold; white satin sleeves, embroidered; scarlet velvet and satin cap; white hose.

C. SMITH, ESQ.
ESQUIRE TO THE KNIGHT OF THE RED ROSE.

The same.

R. MURRAY, ESQ.
ESQUIRE TO THE KNIGHT OF THE RAM.

An Elizabethan costume of blue velvet and white satin, embroidered with silver; blue velvet cloak, lined with crimson; blue cap and plume of white feathers; white silk hose.

R. FERGUSON, ESQ.
ESQUIRE TO THE KNIGHT OF THE RAM.

The same.

HON. MR. CUST,
ESQUIRE TO THE KNIGHT OF THE BLACK LION.

Evening Costume.—A French blue velvet cassock, trimmed with silver gymp lace, the collar turned over with white satin; cap of blue velvet, slashed or puffed with white satin, and ornamented with a blue and white feather, fastened by a jewelled clasp.

HON. MR. GASCOIGNE,
ESQUIRE TO THE KNIGHT OF THE BLACK LION.

Blue velvet tunic, embroidered with silver; vest of silver embroidery; blue cap and white plume; white silk hose.

MARK WHYTE, ESQ.
PAGE TO THE KNIGHT OF THE DRAGON.

Evening Costume.—A black velvet cassock, with the collar turned over with white satin, with a vest of silver tissue; sleeves slashed with white satin; cap of black velvet, puffed with white satin, having a white feather placed gracefully over the left side. The whole dress trimmed with silver gymp lace.

MAJOR WEYMOUTH.

An Elizabethan costume of rich satin and white cachemere, trimmed and embroidered with silver; cap of pink velvet and plume of white feathers.

CAPTAIN BLANE,

An archer's costume of the fifteenth century.

MR. BROWNLOW.

The same.

MR. STUART HAY.

The same.

CAPTAIN MONTGOMERY.

The same.

CLAUDE ALEXANDER, ESQ.
CAPTAIN OF THE AYRSHIRE ARCHERS.

Green velvet, embroidered with gold, of the sixteenth century.

MR. BULKELEY.

A rich doublet of black silk velvet, slashed with crimson satin, edged with gold lace; cap of black velvet, puffed with crimson satin and escaloped with same, with a white feather; large hanging sleeves, doubled with crimson satin, richly embroidered: tight sleeves and vests, light blue silk, figured and embroidered in gold; white satin shirt, worked with gold flowers and plaited; belt and scabbard, black velvet, worked with gold oak-leaves; magnificent gold chain and jewel; hose, on different evenings, of crimson, white, light blue silk; ankle-boots, turned over with crimson silk; or slippers, black velvet, much pointed, embroidered with gold; gauntlets, white kid, gold-worked and fringed.

A. CAMPBELL, ESQ.

A costume of rich marone velvet; the vest puffed with white satin, and embroidered with gold; trunks of the same, slashed with white, with an edging of gold-lace; a cap same colour, and plume of white feathers.

MR. CHARLES MEYNELL.

A costume of the fifteenth century, of light blue velvet, embroidered with silver and trimmed with ermine, the sleeves of rich embroidery; a light blue velvet cap, faced with white satin, and trimmed with silver; plume of white feathers.

MR. MAXWELL ALEXANDER.

An archer's costume.

CAPTAIN BLAIR.

The same.

MR. ALLAN CUNNINGHAM.

The same.

MR. BOSS.

In the costume of Fitz-James.

MR JOHN YUGE BURGESS.

In the Scotch costume of the fourteenth century, in a dress of silk plaid, with a piece-velvet cloak, trimmed with bullion gold; a cap to correspond, with white plumes; white silk hose; with buskins and spurs.

CONCLUDING REMARKS.

SUCH was the Eglinton Tournament, a pageant which, whether we consider the elegance and beauty of its design or the magnificence of its execution, may fairly be said to have eclipsed all others of modern date. Years have passed, and generations have risen, flourished, and decayed in the long space of time which intervenes between the last chivalric exhibition in the reign of the Tudors, and this resuscitation of such gallant sports and pastimes; and years may, perhaps, again elapse, before a nobleman so well qualified as the Earl of Eglinton, to preside over, arrange, and direct, by his knowledge, enterprise, and skill, such joyous and such martial games, shall hereafter be found to uphold them by his munificence and noble bearing: those, then, who were present at this great festival and "passage of arms," may well congratulate themselves on their good fortune. It was not a sight of every day's occurrence, nor an ordinary incident which they were privileged to behold, nor a mere spectacle of lavish expense, which any rich man may command, and of which the recollection is scarcely longer than the event. This "Tournament" was a grand moving picture of the history of the valorous days of Europe. A living representation of the manners, modes, fashions, and thoughts of those who played, in their times, the great parts on the theatre of the world, and whose example it would be well for the present generation if, in many instances, it were more respected and imitated.

The knights and esquires of Poictiers, Agincourt, and Cressy, are no more:

> " Their swords are rust,
> Their bones are dust,
> Their souls are with the Lord we trust."

Nevertheless their memory survives the destruction of the tomb, and their virtues still shine dimly through the obscurity of time, directing those who inherit their names to emulate their great and glorious actions. He, then, who by the removal of such obscurity, has enabled their descendants to more clearly behold their worth, and more accurately to estimate their characters, has well performed the part of a noble of high rank and lineage, by encouraging the cultivation of generous sympathies in the breasts of his cotemporaries, and by affording the present race of the nobility of England a practical lesson of pristine dignity and ancient virtues. To this praise is the Earl of Eglinton entitled. His lordship has, in the words of the most remarkable man of the present day, on a different occasion, "read a great moral lesson," not, perhaps, thought of at the moment it was given, but which can scarcely fail to be productive of good fruits.

Edward III. was well aware of the effects which were produced by Tournaments, and such like valorous displays, on the minds and characters of those who took part in them, and of those by whom they were beheld. That monarch had, besides the mere ostentation of the spectacle, and the amusement and excitement of the moment, ulterior objects in contemplation. His intention was to form the minds and manners of his subjects to patriotic and national symphathies, to instil principles of honorable feeling, and to beget devotion to the public good. It was for this purpose that he celebrated so frequently the Tournaments with which his reign abounded, and it may fairly be concluded, admitting the discrepancy of the manners of his days from ours, that even, in the nineteenth century, a great deal of what was beneficial to our ancestors may, with equal benefit, be repeated for our edification. A brief notice of the character of his reign we extract from Thomas Warton, a faithful chronicler of the events of those days.

" Edward the Third (says this writer) was an illustrious example and patron of chivalry. His court was the theatre of romantic elegance. I have examined the annual rolls of his wardrobe, which record various articles of costly stuffs, delivered occasionally for the celebration of his Tournaments; such as standards, pennons, tunics, caparisons, with other splendid furniture of the same sort: and it appears that he commanded these solemnities to be kept with a magnificence superior to that of former ages, at Lichfield, Bury, Guildford, Eltham, Canterbury, and twice at Windsor, in little more than the space of one year. At his triumphant return from Scotland, he was met by 230 knights at Dunstable, who received their victorious monarch with a grand exhibition of these martial exercises. He established, in the castle of Windsor, a fraternity of twenty-four knights, for whom he erected a round table, with a round chamber, still remaining, according to a similar institution of King Arthur."

This shows the interest which one of the greatest monarchs of England took in these sports, which, in our day, the Earl of Eglinton has attempted to revive, and will serve to remove the objections which the narrow views of mere utilitarians have made to his exertions.

On this head, we can scarcely do better than extract the words of a Morning Journal, which makes these observations on this great Tournament at Eglinton :—

" The attempt to revive, at the present day, the chivalrous pastime of 'the Tournament,' has been derided by the cold 'philosophy' of a money-getting, utilitarian age. Yet, let us ask, are the mass of the people happier because 'the age of chivalry is past,' and, in what was once 'merrie England,' the sordid, heartless, sensual doctrines of utilitarianism have triumphed over sentiment, and nearly extinguished the fine impulses and generous instincts of man's nature?

"Chivalry divorced from the feudal system, of which it was the graceful accompaniment and softening influence, may be thought to be altogether out of place and out of season. What is there in our advanced state of civilization, it may be asked, which can make it desirable to re-introduce its forms and usages,—the inventions of ages comparatively illiterate? We answer that, though the feudal system has vanished, the spirit that tempered its despotism,—that mitigated its ferocity,—that, in an age of comparative darkness, restrained the arm of savage violence, and led power captive in the silken chains of woman's finest influence, may not be without an object to operate upon, and a field for the exercise of its noblest powers.

"If the feudal power was fierce, and rude, and lawless, until chivalry came to subdue its passions beneath the yoke of an artificial refinement, is not the utilitarian age grovelling, mean, and sordid, and does it not require some counteracting influence,—some elevating and inspiring sentiment,—to redeem its character from the debasing bondage of that material 'philosophy' under which the manly virtues, and all those generous energies that exalt and adorn humanity, are fast perishing from the soil of England, where they once flourished in such vigorous luxuriance?

"Is not such a condition of society tending rapidly to realize the melancholy prediction of the poet Goldsmith, who, with the prophetic eye of genius, foresaw the national degeneracy which the present system, then only beginning to develop itself, would eventually produce :—

> ' A time may come, when, stripp'd of all her charms,
> The land of scholars and the nurse of arms,
> Where noble stems transmit the patriot flame,
> Where kings have toil'd, and poets wrote, for fame,
> One sink of level avarice shall lie,
> And scholars, soldiers, kings, unhonour'd die.'

" Of all systems of tyranny, a plutocracy is the most cruel, selfish, and grinding. It is, therefore, that our utilitarian 'philosophers' admire a money government; for they are cold-hearted and unfeeling sensualists, who trample the poor in the dust, and rail at the aristocracy of birth, because it is associated with generous, elevating, and heroic recollections. They despise, or affect to despise, the patriot passion which makes a man prefer his own country, its interests, and its glory, to all others because that passion, whatever it may be, is not a selfish one. To those who have no directing power but selfishness, it costs no struggle of intellect to get rid of the generous attachment, or prejudice, or whatever it is, to one's country. Their cosmopolitism is but the absence of manly sympathy—but the negation of heart—just as latitudinarianism in religion is not a triumph of charity, but a result of cold indifference.

" How can such persons understand the feeling of the Bard, when, in the fervour of a patriot's enthusiasm, he exclaims,—

> ' O, Caledonia ! stern and wild !
> Meet nurse for a poetic child ;
> Land of brown heath and shaggy wood,
> Land of the mountain and the flood—
> Land of my sires—what mortal hand
> Shall e'er untie the filial band
> That binds me to the rugged strand ?'

" Had that Bard himself, the learned, graceful, and impassioned poet of chivalry, lived to see the Tournament revived on the soil of his beloved Caledonia, how would he have welcomed, with the fascinating strains of his magnificent genius, the revival of the chivalrous splendours of the ' olden time.' Then, perhaps, another Canto would have been added to the ' Lay of the Last Minstrel.' Even in the feebleness of old age such an event would

> ' Have lighted up his faded eye
> With all a poet's ecstacy.'

" To view the ' Tournament' merely in the light of a manly exercise and pastime, is it not one which deserves the encouragement of those who are admirers of recreations which strengthen, instead of enervating, the human frame, and teach the noble combination of hardihood of spirit and gentleness of character ? What can be more masculine, adroit, and graceful, than the action and riding of a well-accomplished knight in the enterprise and evolutions of the Tournament ? As an exhibition of mere animal dexterity and prowess, it is a most interesting spectacle; but when there is added to all that, the indispensable accompaniment of the presiding charm of beauty, and the virtuous influence of woman, all civilized men must admit that the interest of the spectacle is greatly enhanced. Even the mighty genius of Milton did homage at the throne of the ' Queen of Beauty,' when he sang of the scenes

> ' Where ladies' eyes
> Rain'd influence, and judged the prize
> Of wit or arms, where all contend
> To win her smile whom all commend.'

" The scene of the Tournament was graced by the fairest women of Scotland, and among them was the noble mother of the chivalrous host. It is not one of the least recommendations of such a scene that it cannot be considered complete without the presiding attractions of the fair sex. And, surely, in all times and countries there has been no such incentive to deeds of high emprise and honourable estimation as the virtuous influence of women.

" The last gleams of chivalry were shed upon a ' maiden reign.' The father of Elizabeth trod the ' field of the cloth of gold ;' and that great Princess spoke as with the lion-heart of real knighthood (if we can apply that word to a woman) when she rode on her splendidly caparisoned steed to Tilbury Fort, and, in addressing her troops while the armada of Spain, then the greatest nation of the earth, threatened her kingdom with extinction, spoke of ' the foul scorn that Spain and Parma should dare to invade her dominions.' But although the age of chivalry may be said to have expired with a maiden reign, let us hope that the attempt which has been made to revive this most manly and beautiful spectacle, may meet with encouragement and success in the reign of our most illustrious Queen and her Royal Consort, who, by the bright example of their domestic virtues, have given a tone to society of the highest possible refinement, and reflected, on the national character and manners, a lustre far exceeding that of any of her predecessors. We should then find that if ever a powerful enemy should again attempt our shores, England would be in a proud position for triumphant resistance by having a nobility not lapped in enervating pleasures, and debased and enfeebled by luxurious indolence, but trained in athletic and masculine exercises, inured to danger, and inspired with that high feeling of honour which caused chivalry to be, of old, ' the nurse of manly sentiment and heroic enterprise.'

And here must end our notices of this great passage of arms. That these are hardly commensurate with the dignity and splendor of the events they have attempted to record, we are fully aware; but we can hope, with confidence, that they will lead our readers to consult the records of former and more able chroniclers of ancient Tilts and Tournaments, that will excite curiosity and create a taste for research. We have written down what we saw, and what we know—if not with judgment, at least with fidelity ; we have recounted no fabulous romance of our own imagination, but have detailed the facts and circumstances of which we were the witnesses, and in the pleasures of which we found participation and delight.

FINIS.

COOK & CO., PRINTERS, 76, FLEET STREET.